Philosophical Issues in the Education of Adults

Philosophical Issues in the Education of Adults

By K H Lawson

CONTINUING EDUCATION PRESS, UNIVERSITY OF NOTTINGHAM

First published in 1998 by
Continuing Education Press
Department of Continuing Education
Education Building
University Park
Nottingham NG7 2RD

© Continuing Education Press
University of Nottingham 1998

ISBN 1 85041 0852

Printed in Great Britain by The Alden Press, Oxford

To Margaret

Contents

Preface   9

Acknowledgements   10

Some key quotations   11

Introduction: The nature and purpose of the collection   13

The Essays:

1. Some problems in the conceptualization of adult education
   for the purposes of research and practice   19

2. Deontological liberalism: the political philosophy of
   liberal adult education   33

3. Liberal education, rule governed behaviour and legal philosophy   43

4. From citizen to self   53

5. The concept of 'moral obligation' as an ethical foundation of
   liberal adult education   71

6. Limits to the concept of 'autonomy' as an adult education objective   85

7. The concepts of 'tradition' and 'translation'   103

8. Rationality, meaning and truth   111

9. 'Intention' and the concept of self-directed learning   127

Bibliography   137

Index   143

Preface

This collection of essays is intended mainly for students and others interested in the theory and practice of adult education. This ambiguous term is set within a framework which I have called 'the liberal tradition' defined in a broader sense than is usually the case. I include the 'great tradition' as defined by H C Wiltshire (1956 and 1976) and also adult education in the North American tradition which has been called 'progressive' and 'humanistic' (J L Elias and Sharon Merrian, 1980). This is influenced by such writers as Dewey, Knowles, Rogers, Taylor, Mezirow and others. This produces a 'broad church' which includes much of what would count as 'adult education' within a liberal democratic society. It should be pointed out however that some of the essays are not uniquely related to adult education in isolation from other forms of education. Adult education has some unique features but it has others in common with all forms of education. Essays 7, 8 and 9 therefore are of more general interest and this is inevitable when deeper philosophical issues are explored. They take us further away from specifics. This does not mean that the content is not relevant to adult education; it is also relevant to adult education.

The main purpose of the essays is to develop a deeper understanding of philosophical issues implicit in theory and practice. The treatment is largely introductory and wider reading is also recommended. There are no direct prescriptions for practice although there are implications for some of the assumptions which underpin it.

Four of the essays have been published previously (see acknowledgments) and they have all developed as a by-product of teaching on courses on adult education. Essays 4 to 9 have been written during the past three years, as teaching texts in the absence of readily accessible material. It is hoped that they might now be useful to a wider audience.

Acknowledgments

I am indebted to the editors and publishers of *The International Journal of Lifelong Education* for permission to reprint the following:

'Deontological liberalism: The political philosophy of liberal adult education' Vol 4, No 3, 1985.

'Liberal education, rule governed behaviour and legal philosophy' Vol 6, No 2, 1987.

'Some problems in the conceptualization of adult education political and ethical concepts and values' Vol 8, No 4, 1989.

I also thank the editor and publishers of *Liberal Adult Education: The End of an Era?* for permission to reprint 'From citizen to self: ethical foundations of liberal adult education', earlier versions of which were presented to a Regional Conference of the Educational Centres Association at Nottingham in 1995 and to the National Conference at Milton Keynes in 1996.

Thanks are also expressed to numerous students who have engaged in discussions on aspects of the essays and to many colleagues for encouragement and support. I thank especially Paula Allman and John Wallis for many hours of constructive and critical discussion. They and Barbara Watts also read early drafts of some of the essays.

I am grateful for constructive comments made by two anonymous referees which have led to changes in the text.

Thanks are also expressed to Heather Blackburn for typing untidy manuscripts so efficiently and to the editorial staff of the Continuing Education Press.

This volume is dedicated to Margaret, my wife, in fulfilment of a long standing promise.

Finally, I must record my pleasure at being able to make use of work published by the late Paul H Grice, my former Oxford tutor. His tutorials were memorable.

Some Key Quotations

'It is significant that we distinguish adult education from other forms of educational provision by reference to the nature of its clients.'

R.W.K. Paterson, 1979

'When I hear terms that have become our hallmark — terms like "self-directed learning" and "ongoing learning" — I am aware that these imply some sort of image of the learner that is libertarian and emergent.'

'If the being of the human being is freedom it is not free-floating freedom, it is as Sartre puts it "freedom in-the-world" '.

Bonnie Barstow, 1984

' . . . the adult as we have said is a mature man, a responsible citizen and a free man.'

'So by "adult education" I shall mean education . . . which in its content organisation and conduct is relevant to and determined by the characteristics of adulthood.'

H.C. Wiltshire, 1966 and 1976

'The idea of self-directed autonomous learning is firmly entrenched in the adult education literature. It is one of only a few core concepts.'

Mark Tennant, 1991

'Texts and teachers play a new role and have secondary significance in this type of education.'

Eduard Lindeman, 1961

'In a modernist story experience signifies convergence to the 'same', the autonomous emancipated "reasonable" person defined by modernity's blueprint, in Postmodern stories it is the signifier of difference and diversity'.

R. Edwards and R, Usher, 1995

'. . . to *think* one is obeying a rule is not to obey a rule. Hence it is not possible to obey a rule "privately", otherwise thinking one was obeying a rule would be the same as obeying it.'

L. Wittgenstein, 1953

'Can there be a private language?'

A. J. Ayer, 1962.

'The picture that emerged did of course represent a whole series of ideas and values drawn from the tradition that gave it birth. It was a picture uniquely suited to liberal democratic societies as they had then developed. If asked to specify what seem to be the main philosophical roots of adult education, I would reply that they are all of the roots that went into the making of liberal democratic societies and that in turn were produced in those societies at various stages in their development.

I shall now attempt to present the outlines of these roots. Before doing so, I wish to make one point that is related to transatlantic differences. I am not talking about liberal education in a sense that implies a particular content, as in a liberal arts course. I mean any content taught or learned in a liberal manner. In this view, even education on reinforced concrete technology can be included. What is important is the emphasis on such things as student choice, critical judgement, flexibility of curriculum, nonauthoritarian organisation, and so on.'

K. H. Lawson, 1991

Introduction: the nature and purpose of the collection

The following collection is designed mainly for an audience within the field of adult education, which as the first essay indicates is an ambiguous concept. It also is an extremely varied field of practice, nevertheless some unity is provided by the assumption that it is a branch of education defined mainly in terms of 'adulthood', the significance of which is illustrated by the 'quotations' which head this volume. 'Knowledge', 'curriculum' and 'teaching' tend to be given second place in the literature where such terms as 'programme', 'self-direction' and 'learning' tend to predominate. Indeed in recent years, the expression 'adult learning' has been used as a replacement for 'adult education', especially by the English National Institute of Adult Education. Typical goals are 'self-actualisation' and 'self-fulfilment' (see W L . Schroeder, 1970) all of which is a recognition of what Kallen (1964) sees in the premise that 'education of the adult is the recognition of his individuality' and is concerned with 'an ongoing process of 'self-differentiation'.' Such phraseology does not constitute definition but it does provide indications of a set of concepts which have a natural home in the traditions of liberal democracy.

As indicated in the preface, these essays focus on 'liberalism' and adult education but the intention is to break away from the traditional liberal studies in the University extramural and WEA sense. It was suggested instead that a broader view might embrace any adult education which embodies liberal values and which is compatible with the principles on which liberal democratic theory is based. Such adult education might be designed to help individuals to understand what liberal democracy implies, how to function within such a system and also how to criticise and recognise its deficiencies. The essays constitute a study of the 'anatomy' of liberalism and adult education in this sense which enables us to embrace what Sharon Merriam (1980) describes as the 'progressive tradition of Dewey, Lindeman, Bergevin and others and the 'humanistic tradition' of such writers as Marlow, Rogers and Knowles, who exposed a student centred andragogical approach. The essays are also intended to demonstrate that although liberalism as a philosophical as well as a political system embodies a conception of 'individuality' that does not necessarily imply a commitment to an ideology of 'individualism'. On the contrary, the essays attempt to show that 'individuality' implies 'mutuality'. One can *only* be an individual in association with other individuals. Conceptually, an individual is seen as a differentiated member of a class or category of 'human beings' who within communities generate cultures which help to define individual members and which embody systems whereby cooperation and mutual regulation are made possible. 'Political and legal' systems, 'ethical codes', 'theories of knowledge', 'conceptions of truth' and above all 'languages' are all examples of 'systems' in the intended sense. Whether they are seen as 'beneficent' or 'malign' in their operation is arguable but whether or not we feel disposed to maintain or to reform the 'liberal' form of life and its institutions, understanding precedes action. It is hoped that the essays might be of use in achieving understanding on the part of adult educators. Whether they choose to maintain or to challenge liberalism as defined is up to them.

The style of argument varies from essay to essay, but they are written from the perspective of the 'analytical' tradition of philosophical thinking. This is not a fashionable approach within adult education although it is well established in the study of child education. Another intention therefore, is to introduce adult educators to a set of ideas which might be new to them but which are common currency elsewhere. A feature of the analytical style is its concentration upon detailed argument within a narrow focus. Conclusions tend to be provisional and revisable although they are sometimes expressed with vigour. This leads to a practice of debate and criticism, and work as it is published is subjected to close scrutiny. In the academic journals, there is a strong tradition of 'comment' and 'rejoinder' not often found in adult education literature. It is true, that in exposition, some writers are quoted as 'authorities' but it is as provisional and conditional authorities that they should be regarded. This seems to be in marked contrast to those in adult education who seem to regard say Gramsci, Freire or Foucault as fixed points of reference rather than as sounding boards against whom other ideas might be tested or contrasted.

In adult education theorising 'critical theory' has become popular (see e.g. Bright, ed., 1989) which from a liberal, analytical point of view, should in turn be subjected to critical analysis rather than be applied *ex cathedra,* as is the work of say Adorno, Habermas, Foucault and others. This is one legitimate tradition but it tends to distort the debate within adult education which in recent years appears to have been dominated by a concern for 'power relationships' as if these were all that mattered. Concepts such as 'truth' and 'knowledge' tend to be denigrated as the product of 'power relationships' (see e.g. Jane L. Thompson ed., 1980) whereas 'truth' is a notion embedded in everyday life. We depend upon it when say, someone tells us that 'the next bus is due in 15 minutes from now'. An analytical understanding of such usage and its semantic foundations seems to be essential. The notion of 'rationality' is questioned also as a 'white male middle class concept' (see for example postmodern literature such as Edwards and Usher, 1995) but it is worth reflecting on the impossibility of language if rationality is not presupposed and these are the kinds of questions raised in these essays because they have educational implications.

It is not claimed that ideas are always politically and ideologically neutral and a thesis implicit in the present collection is that 'liberalism' as a political concept and as a philosophical position or tradition are interrelated. But the traditions go back well before the emergence of a modern style 'middle class'. As one essay (No. 4) illustrates, we are dealing with ideas which have roots in classical Greece where they were worked out in response to concrete political problems. This is true today of Marxism (say) which is one theoretical response to political issues, but it is now a century old and together with liberal ideas, in need of fresh examination in order to attempt to establish what if anything is of transcendent value and what is historically contingent. None of our ideas have quite the meaning developed in their original contexts and today platonic theories of knowledge are seen for what they are (or were) but we still *use* a concept of knowledge. The epistemologies of Locke and Descartes were rooted in individual experience in the case of the former, and individual reflection in the case of the latter. These are now shown to be defective in a number of respects, but they helped to establish a culture of 'individuality' in historic struggles against e.g. the authority of church dogma and out of the complex conditions of the English civil war. Power struggles play a part but they are not the whole of the story.

A postmodern response might be that a radical break in our long traditions is now taking place. This may or may not be true. It is a matter of interpretation. But if true, the implications are profound and in need of critical examination because they question concepts which have become almost universal. 'Truth' is one example already mentioned, others include 'justice', 'rights', 'duties' and 'obligation'. Can there be a society which denies them because they form part of a system of rationality? A 'radically situated', 'free floating' or 'decentred' individual might be put forward as new ideals but are they consistent with the idea of a *society* which in liberal terms is based upon mutuality? Can there be a society without 'mutuality'?

These are all philosophical as well as political issues and as such they are at the heart of what some of us regard as 'adult education' seen as a process of enquiry and criticism as opposed to say, prescription and indoctrination or simply as the development of employable skills and competencies. My preference is for the 'enquiry and criticism option' and this is what I understand liberal education to be. But, there can be no premature closures. The debate must be kept open. On the other hand, and this is the central question which the following essays raise, are there some points which *are* fixed? There are different explanations of 'truth', 'meaning' and so on and there are different conceptions of rationality. But however they are defined can these *concepts* be dispensed with if we are to retain social institutions of *some* kind, including adult education?

The Essays

Each in turn concentrates upon a specific theme or group of ideas, some of which receive more attention than others. Subsidiary themes in each essay then become major themes in others. Overlap is therefore intentional and it is used as a heuristic device, in order to demonstrate how concepts and themes interrelate and reappear in various contexts. In some cases also, a concept is analysed more extensively in a subsequent essay because such analysis would appear as an unwieldy digression when first referred to in earlier essays where it would obscure the main thrust of an argument. It is also hoped that repetition from various vantage points might be an aid to understanding.

Essays 2 to 6 explore political and ethical concepts and values in the liberal tradition within which liberal adult education (as defined in the preface) is located. The tradition may be seen as embodying a constructive tension between the concepts of individuality and society.

Essay No. 1

This deals in a broad way with the problems involved in conceptualising adult education and it also introduces a number of concepts and values which form the subject matter of subsequent essays, most of which were prompted by the writing of the first essay although essays Numbers 2 and 3 predate it.

The concepts introduced include 'rationality' and 'rule governance', 'obligation', 'autonomy', 'translation', 'rationality', and 'intention'. It is recognised that these subjects impinge upon other branches and forms of education but an attempt is made to indicate their particular relevance to 'adult education' which in the author's view cannot be detached totally from other concepts of 'education'. To some extent this is now recognised in the conjunction 'adult and continuing education'.

Essay No. 2
The starting point is the philosophy of individualism implicit in liberal adult education which is then put into the context of the political philosophy of liberalism from Locke to Rawls and Nozick. In the concluding paragraphs, the idea of the 'social self' is introduced and it is presented as a challenge to adult education.

Essay No. 3
This essay takes up the concepts of 'justice', 'rights' and 'rules' as public regulators of private behaviours and corporate behaviour. The ideas of 'intentionality' and 'rationality' are introduced together with 'freedom' and 'autonomy'. These ideas relate directly to themes in the previous essay. Legal theory is introduced because 'law' and the interpretation of law provides paradigms of the idea of 'rule governance' and problems associated with it. In sum 'rules' are seen as essential to the idea of 'freedom' and a liberal society. The concept of 'rule governance' appears later in discussions on 'autonomy', 'language' and 'rationality'.

Essay No. 4
A number of themes from Essay No. 2 are taken up again and developed in a discussion of 'ethical foundations'. A number of ideas are traced from their historical roots and the concept of a 'tradition' is introduced and it is argued that this provides ethical foundations. In the liberal tradition, a concept of 'individuality' is seen as a keystone and it has produced a logic of choice based on the premise that 'I want' has a greater claim than 'I ought'. This it is suggested is built into adult education theory and practice. The next essay on 'moral obligations' suggests an alternative ethical foundation.

Essay No. 5
This essay takes the principle of 'student choice' as a starting point and sees it as providing a solution to the question 'what ought adults to learn' without prescribing a curriculum. This in effect presupposes an ethic which does not embody any idea of 'the good' beyond that of individual choice. The difficulties inherent in such a view are considered in the light of the concept of 'citizenship' which carries obligations, and the principle of 'rule governance' reappears. The general conclusion is that individual choices have to be justified in a communal context by the giving of 'good reasons' for what is chosen.

Essay No. 6
The previous essay has implications for the concept of 'autonomy' in adult education. It is argued that we function with a limited, constrained concept of 'autonomy'. The constraints, following the previous essay are partly 'political',

partly 'legal' and partly 'moral' but following Wittgenstein on 'language and meaning' it is argued that there are logical constraints. Questions are considered related to concepts of 'individuality' and the concept of 'intentionality'. The latter is analysed in more detail in Essay No. 9.

The three final essays are different in style and they explore 'rationality', the semantics of 'communication' as a central educational process and the concept of 'intention' as a component in the idea of 'rational self direction' as an adult education concept.

Essay No. 7

The main theme is an analysis of the concept of 'tradition', especially as embodied in languages each of which *is* a tradition. In learning and in communicating we are involved in processes of 'translation' and 'interpretation' either between 'natural' languages such as English, French or Urdu, and between 'technical' languages such as 'physics', 'psychology' etc. which have a distinctive vocabulary and concepts. The 'problem of translation' is fundamental to 'understanding how we understand' and communicate. This is a very introductory essay and it should be read in conjunction with the next essay.

Essay No. 8

The concepts of 'rationality', 'meaning' and 'truth' are fundamental to all education. It is therefore highly relevant to adult education but not specific to it. The essay discusses 'rational action', 'rationality' and 'choice', 'rule based rationality', 'scientific rationality' and then moves on to language as a paradigm of a rational system and introduces 'intention, 'meaning' and 'communication'. This essay is of general educational interest but it should be of specific interest to adult educators working in multi-cultural societies.

Essay No. 9

This essay returns to the concept of 'intention' and extends the brief discussion in Essay No. 6. The concept is considered for its relevance to 'self-directed learning' but 'intention' is shown to be of importance to our understanding and explanation of key concepts such as 'truth', 'meaning', 'beliefs' and the idea of 'a conceptual scheme' as embodied in language.

1
Some problems in the conceptualization of adult education for the purposes of research and practice

Introduction

This essay is concerned initially with two questions:

1) As organizers of adult education, how do we determine what kinds of activity we should be organizing and for what purposes?

2) As researchers into adult education, how do we delimit the range of phenomena which is our legitimate area of concern?

Put more generally, the questions may be rephrased as the single question, is there an identifiable domain of adult education, defined in terms of its practices and purposes, researchable in ways such that a distinct discipline of adult education can emerge which is informed by its own distinctive theory?

We are therefore concerning ourselves with definitions of adult education for the purposes of practice and theory.

The diversity of practice

Writers such as Wiltshire (1964), Lawson (1975) and Paterson (1979) have each tried to identify a unique concept of adult education by drawing on the two discrete concepts of education and adulthood. It is now recognised, however, that adulthood is a normative concept, definable more readily in terms of values and status than in positivistic terms. The concept of education most heavily drawn upon was that of liberal education which in recent years has been questioned on philosophical and political grounds as an adequate representation of what is meant by education. The upshot has been, however, to regard university extramural and WEA type classes as the paradigm of adult education.

Even in 1970, John Lowe took the British to task for taking too narrow a view of what constituted adult education to the 'deplorable neglect of the education of adults as a whole' (1970:23). Within the LEA sector alone, Lowe's survey included colleges of further education and community associations along side the more obvious candidates such as evening institutes and educational centres. His survey of the education of adults, as he preferred to call it, included the armed forces, prisons, Women's Institutes, Townswomen's Guilds, employers, industrial training boards, rural music schools, the Field Studies Council, broadcasting, films, as well as libraries, museums, and art galleries and political parties, to mention only a few. In the 1990s, additional candidates might be the Manpower Services Commission, the Health Council, the Open University, the Sports Council, the National Consumer Council and many others (see the NIACE Year Book).

It seems unlikely that many people would now question that all of the above organisations, and no doubt many others, are involved in adult education in some sense of the term. It seems questionable, however, whether all can be embraced within a single unifying concept, philosophy or theory. Some of the examples might best be seen as being in the business of communication, others in training and some in propaganda and indoctrination. But the very act of making such distinctions begs questions about the meaning of education.

The plea for overall conceptualization has often be made. Lowe himself asked for 'a descriptive method which will present the field as nearly as possible as a whole and show the relationship between one kind of activity and another' (1970:29). Earlier still, the outlines of an emerging field of university study had been sought (Jensen, et al. 1964) and the pleas for unity is still present in a paper on the 'undisciplined discipline' (Plecas and Sork 1986).

The issues are not merely of academic interest for the purposes of research; they are of importance to organisers and trainers of professionals who need to know what they are being trained for.

Part of the problem lies in the fact that educational phenomena as manifest in practices and institutions are social constructs, and they change. They are not natural in the way that the objects of the physical sciences are (although the epistemological and ontological status of physical phenomena is not without ambiguity). Perceptions of education (and other social phenomena) change and vary according to the observers, who bring with them conceptual frames of reference which define both what they look at and what they look for. In turn, practices change and new ones are introduced in the wake of new or changing conceptualization. The field under review responds to new conceptualization, therefore there exists what might be called systematic instability or variability. The problem is how to cope with it, describe and research it, organize within the field and train people for work in it.

Formulating the problem

A number of assumptions are made by those who ask for a discipline of adult education, one of which is the obvious — there is a domain of adult education if only we can find it. But, unlike the explorer who assumes that there is a source of the Nile in a particular geographical region, we cannot, in the same manner, verify our claim to have found our quarry without first defining it. The trouble is, we do not know quite how to start.

A phenomenalist might say, 'look at the phenomena' and so might a natural scientist, who would then begin to formulate theories and fresh hypotheses for further investigation. But the scientist knows that he is looking at, say, bird behaviour or plants. There is already a preconceptualization of both bird and behaviour, although further refinement might be possible and one could, perhaps, distinguish between, say, behaviour and intentional action.

In the case of adult education there are two issues. The potential range of phenomena is large. It could be infinitely large: therefore we require criteria for delimiting our area of concern.

Why is this example but not that example significant? This is a question which cannot be avoided, but to whom or to what do we turn for an answer? The discipline of history, sociology, or what? Could there be a distinct discipline of education or of adult education, or is there merely a field or domain which is cross-referenced and identified by an amalgam of other disciplines? The practical answer is probably the latter and there is a strong tradition of the history, sociology, psychology and philosophy of education and adult education. These severally and jointly contribute to a study of the subject, but how do we define that subject? We might therefore be pushed back to the evolution of practices and concepts over time as an aspect of general history out of which something called education (or its analogue in languages other than English) emerged.

However, whatever through time has been called education does not necessarily help us to identify what might have been called education at any given point. Lowe's strictures on adult education are a good example. Do we regard as adult education in the 1930s or the 1960s only what was then regarded as such?

We have here a problem common to all attempts to define according to historically or culturally relative contexts. We are operating in the present, as were our forebears in, say, the 19th or early 20th century, for whom education, adult education or whatever, is an immediate issue. The immediate and historically relative context has to be or is likely to be perceived, interpreted and understood against acquired experience and ideas. The present is categorized and conceptualized in the light of what seems to be the best fit, drawn from earlier thinking. Inevitably, the meanings of words change in some degree but the present example under review is, in some respects, regarded as an example of a certain kind. This, at least, is one view which is based on a historicist epistemology.

What is being dealt with is the general problem of applying universals to concrete examples, which rapidly takes us into a consideration of the structure and function of language and a philosophical consideration of the nature and logical status of universals. How do we judge what is the correct appropriate application of a given term in different cultural and historical contexts? Opinions on this vary. The possibility of a foundational philosophy which provides a basis for rational thought and discourse (on, say, Cartesian or Kantian lines) is not currently fashionable, and is indeed dismissed by writers such as Richard Rorty (1979). Philosophy, in his view, is not concerned with the search for the foundations of thought. It has become instead a discursive interpretive dialogue in which there are no firm criteria, least of all criteria available in some privileged way to philosophers.

A number of thinkers taking up Wittgenstein's theory of language games, each self-contained and incommensurable (i.e. untranslatable in terms of each other) and encouraged by Rorty's arguments, have opted for relativism as the only possible valid standpoint. If they are right, then there seems to be little possibility of constructing a domain of adult education, a philosophy of adult education or a theory of adult education because we are denied the possibility of universalizing or generalizing beyond particular cultural or time-bound contexts unless of course adult education constructs its own self-contained language game.

Such a move would be consistent with Hirst's forms of knowledge argument which has in recent years been of considerable influence within the liberal tradition (Hirst, 1965, 1974, 1983). His view is that knowledge is located within a number of distinct disciplines, each with its own conceptual framework, its own tests of assertability and methods of validation. Hirst's classification does not, however, include such fine distinctions as education, which is merely subsumed under the human sciences.

Following Hirst, therefore, we have the amalgam of discipline problem to contend with and, within it, the task of identifying and defining a domain of adult education. Evidence suggests that not much progress is being made and that a pernicious relativism persists.

The problem described

Plecas and Sork (1986) try to describe the state of adult education as a discipline from a North American point of view. They see the onset of an illness in the field of research and theory construction, and a number of symptoms or tendencies are identified:

1)   There is a tendency to interpret differential effects (e.g. of educational techniques) 'as an opportunity to create nominal variables' and to see

'any newly discovered relationship between any two variables . . . as a basis for a new sub-discipline' (1986: 49, 50).

2)   There is an insistent belief that the phenomenon under study is something other than it really is, 'which leads to a refusal to work within an existing paradigm' and to 'an insistence that new paradigms are needed' (p.50).

3)   As a consequence, there is a failure to build upon (as opposed to beside) the work of others (p.53).

4)   New terms such as gerogogy, eldergogy and synergogy follow on the heels of Knowles' andragogy and ever more discrete subgroups are identified, each with its own techniques and concept of what it means to educate an adult (or at least a particular kind of adult).

On the British side of the Atlantic there are similar manifestations, although they are expressed more in terms of practice than theory. Instead of mainstream adult education, as a focus of interest (and funding), we now have special provision for disadvantaged groups, and particular methods and curricula are beginning to emerge. There is women's education, Black education, education for the socially disadvantaged, and so on. Whether or not these examples are really distinct it is perhaps too early to say, but one is left with a feeling that adult education is receding into the mist.

This feeling is reinforced by the appearance of new concepts, such as community, lifelong, recurrent and continuing education, although here too, the differences might be more nominal than substantive.

However, the proponents of new terms claim to be offering something new and their avowed aims are often expressed in socio-political terms, rather than in the overt language of education. Examples of these claims and their implications are considered below.

Changing aims and changing concepts in the education of adults.

Recurrent education has been referred to as 'the first new idea in education this century' (Houghton and Richardson 1974:6), but at one level it might seem that they are doing no more than putting forward changes in organization and delivery systems which will articulate educational processes in a rational way throughout life. One intention is to bridge the gap between school and post-school, and to shift emphasis away from the former to the latter. In recommending this change of emphasis, more fundamental implications are entailed. Devolution of decision-making, the decay of institutional autonomy and the abolition of curriculum teaching are elements in a total programme. The first of these is an extension of the idea of individual autonomy, which is an element in liberal theory, but as an extension of democratic principles it becomes a political aim. Curriculum teaching is seen as having a particular epistemological base which must be questioned and there are implications for teaching and learning. Both how and what questions are involved.

A strictly educational approach could be seen as concentrating on the curriculum issue, which has implications for the manner in which learning is undertaken and for the content of learning. It is clear, however, that in the recurrent education philosophy the division between social and political issues on the one hand and educational aspects on the other is untenable. It becomes difficult to decide, therefore, whether we are being asked to consider a new concept of education for both adults and children, a new philosophy or ideology of education within which a concept (new or old) is embedded, or a new view of society in which education has a more central role.

Plecas and Sork suggest that adult education researchers should single out the notion of organized learning as the primary phenomenon in adult education and concentrate upon 'instructional processes intended to bring about learning' (1985:59). What they ignore is the philosophical and conceptual framework within which these ideas derive their meaning. The concept of instruction vanishes in recurrent education, and the conception of what is learned is different - not just a different selection of knowledge but an epistemologically different type of knowledge.

We must ask therefore whether it is meaningful or significant to research learning under two diverse systems in the hope of comparing effectiveness, because different criteria of effectiveness seem to be called for. For the organizer, also, the choices become too fundamental to allow us to regard, say, recurrent and liberal education as alternative ways of arriving at similar ends. The ends themselves are different.

The objection may be made that recurrent education does not exist except as a theory (in a loose sense of the term): therefore alternative phenomena do not come within the researcher's purview. On the other hand, we might wish to consider seriously whether, for example, recurrent education ought to be introduced: therefore criteria for comparison are necessary.

Examples of community education are available, but here it is not easy to determine whether traditional goals are being sought within new contexts or whether a radically different concept of education is involved. There are many differences in practice under the same name and there is a gap between the rhetoric and practice. I have argued elsewhere (Lawson 1982) that writers on community education are concerned with a number of issues and consequently have a number of goals, but it is difficult to pinpoint a single consensual view.

The following features may be identified in varying degrees:
1)   There is an emphasis on developing a sense of community as a social ideal.

2)   The community is perceived as an ideal unit within which individuals can contribute to decision making.

3)   Community education as a participative activity is a means of overcoming a perceived lack of relevance on the part of more traditional forms of education.

4)   Tackling the issues set out in (1) to (3) above will *ipso facto* tackle problems of inequality of access to education.

In practice, however, much that is provided as community education is not significantly different from more traditional provision. This suggests that actual perceptions on the ground do not necessarily coincide with newly introduced concepts. This raises interesting questions about the dynamics of change and the relationships between ideas and practice, but our immediate concern is with the new concepts, of which community education is an example, and the older terms education and adult education. What precisely is the logical and epistemological status of terms such as education and adult education in the first place?

The problem can be presented in terms of the relationship between the subsets of a partitioned set, each of which has an equivalence relationship which defines it as part of the set. In other words, why is adult education called adult *education* and why is it called *adult* education? Similar questions can be asked of lifelong, recurrent and continuing education. What binds them together? Is educational discourse an identifiable language game and are the other qualified forms distinct or related?

The answers given to such questions will determine our views on whether there is or can be a unifying philosophy or theory (we ignore the distinction for the moment) of either education or adult education, or does each newly identified or newly invented sector, with its own concepts, require its own philosophy or theory?

The conclusion that we are dealing with separate and discrete areas and concepts would be consistent with the current intellectual climate, which seems to be predisposed to various forms of historical, cultural or subcultural relativism and concept relativism. This is the philosophical equivalent of 'each doing his or her own thing' and the associated rejection of normative criteria by which to judge behaviour. Whether or not we are dealing with symptoms or causes is not clear, but a lack of consensual agreement in many areas of human conduct seems to be widespread.

In many ways the current intellectual climate can be seen as a direct outcome of the liberal tradition itself. This tradition is anti-authoritarian, it encourages ongoing criticism and the emergence of new ideas. It encourages what is termed individual autonomy, although this concept is itself in need of critical analysis.

Taken together, the cluster of ideas associated with liberalism presuppose the fundamental assumption that no one can define the good for another (see Lawson 1985). This may be extended to include 'truth' as well as 'good', and in practice the assumption is taken into many areas such as music, and the arts generally. It also permeates adult education philosophy and practice where student choice and the democratic definition or construction of knowledge are in danger of becoming dogmas. These ideas are implicit in andragogy, recurrent education and what is termed radical adult education, as well as in traditional WEA practice, albeit in a weaker form.

This should not imply that such ideas are wrong and questions might be better asked of them in terms of to what extent they are or should be incorporated into our thinking and practice. In asking questions such as these, we are well on the way to reintroducing (unfashionable) normative ideas, but if we do so, we are equally obliged to examine the roots of normative philosophy and theory.

The philosophical issues

In trying to establish the theoretical basis of a normative adult education theory and practice (a 'philosophy' in the sense of an ' ideology') we have to face up to the question of what, if anything, exists as a 'valid' philosophy as an analytical tool or a source of our philosophy in the first sense.

It is here that we find further lack of unity on what constitutes philosophical method or the nature of philosophy itself. The history of philosophy is full of attempts to establish the foundation of thought, but it seems difficult in the end to escape the conclusion that our particular problems, as addressed in the present paper, are essentially linguistic in character.

What we are presently seeking is a set of sentences containing the terms 'education' and 'adult' (both separately and in conjunction) such that they might be meaningfully used. Any knowledge claims contained in these sentences have to be capable of being rightly or justifiably asserted. There has to be something to which 'education', 'adult' and 'adult education' refer, but the reference cannot be other than linguistically defined.

We cannot fall back upon the observation conditionals of empiricism and physical science as being foundational because, as had been argued above, what we observe appears to be determined in a strong sense by our linguistic- and value-based framework. In other words, observation presupposes concep- tualization. There is no observation claim which entails a given set of descrip- tive sentences $S_1, S_2, S_3 \ldots S_9$ because these descriptive sentences are them- selves logically related, $S_1, S_2, S_3 \ldots S_{n-1}$, in such a way that they define S_n which is the observation claim itself. The process is circular. Once defined in general or universal terms, any given observation entails a given set of descriptive sentences or it does not. We either verify an observation or we do not. But if this is so, can we ever move away from a given standard case or paradigm?

A cat is a cat, and adult education is adult education, without variation. But there are many kinds of cat and we are in the end dealing with penumbra problems as defined in legal theory (see Lawson, 1987). Laws and rules are not applied algorithmically, they are applied interpretively. Can we say the same thing with concepts?

Where abstract concepts such as 'knowledge', 'equality',' learning' and the like are concerned, the notion of reducing them to observation claims cannot apply and these apply to education only insofar as institutions and practices are involved. Arguments about the nature of knowledge or the nature and purpose of education or what it means for something or someone to be adult in character are inevitably linguistic. Justificatory rather than observational claim therefore becomes the relevant terminology. We seek substantiating claims rather than verifying statements.

A possible way forward which does not restrict us to a relativist view, which in the end confines us solipsistically within a personal cultural and epistemological box, seems to be desirable, and for a number of reasons.

Relativism in the end seems to be self-refuting or retorsive in character (it bends back upon itself). The crudest form of argument which demonstrates this is as follows:

The claim that 'X' is meaningful only in relation to a particular culture can be truthfully claimed only within the speaker's culture. If true, then it is false, or at least the claim cannot be put forward as a universal truth. To insist that one's own culture is the source of truth is illogical in that it denies the (relativist) claim being made.

Logical refutation is unlikely to convince the committed relativist because relativism is a view which is now embedded in the current intellectual climate. It is consistent with too many aspirations and values to make it unacceptable. In some ways, relativism encourages pluralistic values but it has probably surfaced at the present time because of the apparently increasing pluralism of our society. Community groups and minorities based on race, religion, sexual orientation and so on, are fashionable foci of discussion and political activism and it is in their individual interest to claim that they have their own subculture value systems, their own standards of validity, significance, and so on.

Some would see all this as a symptom of a disintegrating society (see, for example, MacIntyre, 1981) but the attempt to define subcultures and community relationships can also be seen as an antidote to extreme individualism on the one hand and the dehumanizing effect of large-scale social organizations on the other. It is a good question, therefore, whether such aspirations should be criticized because they are in some sense irrationally based. This is a serious question because the relativist position in the end is a challenge to the idea of rationality. That a belief is good on short-term perceptions of immediate pragmatic importance is deemed to be of greater importance than a coherent philosophical foundation. We find philosophers such as Rorty (1979, 1987) talking of having arrived at a 'post philosophical culture', and in asking whether such a culture is desirable Rorty asks, 'Can the ubiquity of language ever really be taken seriously? Can we see ourselves as never encountering reality *except under a chosen description?* ' (Rorty 1987:57).

The emphasis should be upon the phrase, 'chosen description'. Is it really a question of individual or group choices on pragmatic criteria relevant only to their interests and situation or should we continue to seek more general criteria by means of which to judge the validity of individual and group choices? This is precisely the philosophical point at issue and which is often fiercely contested. One way of presenting it is to ask, Can there be overriding meta philosophy or universal principles? The question often appears to emerge, however, as a moral question of the form, Ought there to be, or is it right there should be any overriding general principles? We seem to be culturally predisposed to reject the idea and to refuse to assess it on general rational grounds because it is believed that such grounds do not exist.

If we lock ourselves into a set of beliefs against the possibility of rational principles, the consequences need careful consideration. On the other hand, it can be argued that whatever the philosophical base, practice — historically and in the present — contains more irrational elements than might be supposed. However, if a form of cultural relativism or concept relativism is accepted, each new manifestation in the field of education could be seen as discrete from and incommensurable with what has gone before. Each new '-gogy' or '-ism' is seen as meaningful only on its own terms. No general theorising would be possible or acceptable, and there would be no basis on which to compare systems and concepts. However, we are in danger of contradicting ourselves because the claim made is tantamount to stating that in principle there can be no intercomparison, but such a claim is disallowed if relativism is correct. The problem of universal ability still hovers in the background.

It has been suggested that many of the ideas in vogue have derived, in part at least, from Wittgenstein's language games as discrete and incommensurable, but if languages are part of a partitioned set, some resemblance to a more general conception of language must be discoverable, and we are pushed back to general theories of meaning. This is not the place to tackle such a large issue head on but it might be noted that a good deal hangs on the definition of a 'game' and, within games, mini games which share some, but not all, the defining characteristics of the main category. There is language and by parity of reasoning there are sub-languages, within which there might be identifiable mini languages. What relates, say, German and English, and what relates dialects to the parent stem? What relates all languages in this sense to the 'language' of, say, mathematics and what links mathematics to physics, particle physics to other branches? It is a commonplace that intercommunication within the sciences is becoming restricted within very narrow specialist sub-sciences, yet they are each recognized as science.

Is the difficulty of intercommunication a result of incommensurability or simply of the contingent difficulty of each of us learning more than a limited range of languages?

The Hirst view of knowledge implies a version of concept relativism which functions with conceptually different forms of knowledge, e.g. physical sciences, human sciences, history, religion, etc. Each is deemed to have its own 'particular concepts and criteria of judgement' (Hirst 1974:46). Some of us ('educated people') operate in all these fields, albeit at an elementary level in many cases, therefore on this argument we cannot make sense or construct a unity out of our own varied experience. Yet in all the examples given by Hirst there is something identifiable as 'knowledge'. A formal logical definition hovers in the background. Does this imply that despite *prima facie* difficulties in reconciling say scientific thought and knowledge with religious experience and knowledge, a solution is possible?

Are there ways forward?

Are there ways forward? A negative answer may be seen as pessimistic but inevitable, which leads to a view of society where no general idea of 'the good' is possible, and which can have no overall vision. In many ways this is the position that we are already in and it helps to explain the phenomenon of undisciplined disciplines. The same position may also be seen as liberating.

A negative answer might not be inevitable, however, but what we wish to avoid is probably a return to an unduly constricting meta-philosophy which in political terms can be translated into authoritarian dogma.

Our liberal antecedents rebel against such notions. The specification therefore reduces to a balance between discipline and freedom and between order and disorder. Freedom becomes freedom within a framework which itself has to be flexible.

One possible way forward is suggested by several writers, among whom Hilary Putnam and Glenn Langford are examples.

Langford (1985) tries to root educational discourse in the idea of tradition. Putnam (1982, 1987) draws upon similar ideas and points out the relationship between the transcendent and the immanent.

For Langford, educators work within a tradition which gives meaning to such terms as 'teacher' and 'teaching'. It is a tradition in which theory or philosophy and practice are intertwined and Langford claims that 'a philosophy of education is itself part of the practice' (1985:50). A tradition, therefore, can be regarded as a mixture of ideas and practice which, as we noted earlier, inform and modify each other. Langford draws upon Gombridge's notion of style in art where, despite individual variation, a history of the development of style is describable. We can generalise from this and say that there can be no definable history of anything without an identifiable unifying theme which helps to define the sense of style. Langford illustrates his point about art by stating 'Clearly there could be no tradition — or history of art — if painters such as Giotto and Constable had not painted pictures on particular dateable occasions' (1985:21). Tradition is, therefore, made by a succession of concrete events, participants in which build upon and modify the work of predecessors, either immediate or in the more distant past. Peers at given points either copy or distance themselves from each other but such may be seen as a variation around a style or a set of norms. Tradition in this light is seen as helping to develop individuality, and it actually gives meaning to individuality and creates the possibility of change by offering ways of seeing and doing, either as a guide or as a point of departure. Tradition puts each of us into a social context within which individual perceptions, interests and intentions can be judged, both by ourselves and others.

Putnam's arguments seem to run in the same grain. He tries to rescue thought from the solipsism to which relativism logically leads and he stresses the importance in each concrete instance where attempts to establish meaning are immanent in the immediate situation. We also have to take into account the transcendent which is outside the immediate situation (see Putnam 1982, 1987). Behind every attempt to justify a concrete knowledge claim or to give reasons for action there are presuppositions about, for example, the possibility of knowledge, reason and justification. These are seen as transcendental regulators which influence but do not narrowly determine meaning in the concrete situation. These are models or paradigms to use as points of reference from which to start and against which the extent of our modification of concepts may be assessed.

In this way we are moving towards the Hermeneutical approach of Gadamer et al, which sees interpretation of the present in the light of the past and vice versa. Linguistic contact is maintained through time and within time and this makes communication possible.

Of course, we can be accused of restating the relativist's position. We are confined within a tradition which is a particular culture existing through time. On the other hand the tradition may be so widely defined that it embraces a very wide range of human experience. Consider, for example, how widely the net has to be cast in order to encapsulate Western culture: it takes us at least into the early civilizations in the Middle East, and there seems to be no difficulty in maintaining communication and understanding (via texts and surviving artefacts) over large tracts of time. It is not contingently true to claim that on such a large canvas, subcultures defined by time or place have incommensurable languages and ideas. Translation is possible, albeit with difficulty.

The study of ideas and institutions is therefore possible on a comparative basis and, given the effort, subcultures can understand each other even though they might disagree on points of practice or on intentions.

To return to education and adult education, we have traditions, models, or paradigms with which to start and from which to depart. The distances travelled in individual cases can be assessed and their significance and possible consequences can be evaluated. If old distinctions (e.g. between education and training, or between beliefs and knowledge) are obliterated, it seems possible to judge the validity of doing so against a complex of values, ideas, institutions and practices developed in concrete situations at one level (the immanent) but in a context of tradition (the transcendent) which we simply cannot (logically) ignore because it furnishes us with our modes of perception, understanding and communication at the most universal and at the most particular level.

A domain of adult education and associated theories and philosophies become flexible concepts and both study and practice is within a context of debate, reassessment and redefinition. Paradigms exist and modified ones are created, but each then enters into something like Popper's 'third world of knowledge' which makes its own claims upon the present because we cannot escape from it except by abandoning all claims to rationality.

It will probably be said that the above conclusions lead to further exclusion of philosophy, or at least to an assimilation of philosophy to historical and comparative cultural studies. This is not intended and philosophy as a mode of study is seen as returning to something akin to Wittgenstein's therapeutic role.

Philosophy is again seen as the analysis of concepts and the identification of underlying values. It is still a second-order study of usage. Any further study which draws upon other disciplines is beyond philosophy.

To the extent that the meanings of words and the connotations of concepts change, analysis can never be complete. Theories of meaning and of language will no doubt also continue to change, therefore philosophy itself might best be seen as a process, the purpose of which is to formulate the broadest generalisations possible at any given time relating to such topics as meaning, reason, rationality, justice, knowledge and so on, which are themselves continually woven into the tradition of discourse which they help to define.

To conclude, we return briefly to the problems in generating an adult education theory. What we seem to arrive at is a set of paradigms which can be used as reference points but which change through time, and in the light of which further linguistic and practical recommendations might be judged. We can ask of new additions to the vocabulary and new practices, how they relate to or differ from the old. What old distinctions are blurred, what new distinctions are made and why? Where are we dealing with new methods and new goals, and where are new methods designed only to achieve existing goals? Do new attempts to conceptualize knowledge and learning raise epistemological and practical issues? What is the interplay with social and political values, and so on? A whole research agenda begins to emerge and if testable hypotheses are generated out of such questioning and research, there might be the beginnings of a general theory. Such a theory would itself be contestable and subject to frequent revision.

2

Deontological liberalism: the political philosophy of liberal adult education

Introduction

A philosophy of individualism runs through liberal adult education. It can be seen in such educational goals as personal development and the idea of developing 'autonomous man'. It is implicit in the vocabulary of 'educational rights' and in claims for 'equality of educational opportunity'.

For some, this philosophy represents a strength while for others such as Colin Griffin (1983) and Neil Keddie (1980) the 'ideology of individualism' is a matter for reproach and criticism. Such criticism must be taken seriously as a challenge at the theoretical level and one which is as important as the more practical challenges to liberal adult education such as the withdrawal of public funds and the growing emphasis upon vocational education.

In the older traditions of adult education there was a strong 'utilitarian' element in the ideal of social purpose, the furtherance of social progress and the enhancement of the public good. More recently, however, there have been signs of a significant shift away from utilitarian forms of liberalism and liberalism in the Greek tradition based on the idea of the pursuit of 'the good'. There has instead been a movement towards a 'deontological' type of liberalism which is highly individualistic in character and which is based upon the ideas of 'rights' and 'justice'. It is a philosophy which denies that there can be a general, as distinct from a private, idea of 'the good'.

Deontological liberalism can now be seen as the dominant political and ethical philosophy underpinning liberal adult education and which provides much of its theoretical base. This paper is an attempt to explore the connections between adult education and its underlying philosophy.

The deontological tradition is not new. It goes back at least to John Locke in the seventeenth century but it has been very influentially restated by John Rawls, (1972) and by Richard Nozick (1974) and it is the ideas of these writers that form the main subject for discussion.

The 'individual' in adult education

In a direct and obvious sense, it is individuals who are educated and this is likely
to be denied only by those who believe that in some sense it is the 'community'
or 'social classes' which are the subject of education. 'Education', according
to Paterson (1979: 15)

> 'directly touches us in our personal being, tending our identity at its roots
> and ministering directly to our condition as conscious selves aspiring in all
> our undertakings to a greater fullness and completeness of being.'

Although autonomy is fundamental to deontological liberalism, it does not
exclude the possibility of people agreeing on a particular policy. This happens
when they combine for the purpose of defence or to provide common welfare
services, but what they choose is irrelevant except insofar as it is an expression
of free choice and conducive to the self-interest of each member of the group.
Having chosen, the central concern is for the maintenance of their individual
rights. Fairness as a regulating principle for the regulation of conduct and
transactions between individuals or between individuals and the State is what
really matters from the deontological point of view. This means that, in the last
resort, whatever policy has been agreed upon by members of a group must be
sacrificed if any individual is treated unjustly in order to maintain the policy.

Such a view is by no means as unrealistic as it might appear and it is
exemplified in the argument that public expenditure should not be financed out
of higher taxes on individuals even if some vital service such as education has
to be cut as a consequence. In many respects, the deontological principle is
operative in Britain under the present (1985) government. The case against
taxation is presented in terms of its disincentive effects on effort or on
investment but the claim in effect is that of Nozick who argues that it is a
violation of a person's rights if he is forced to do certain things. In his view,
'the State may not use its coercive apparatus for the purpose of getting some
citizens to aid others'. For Nozick (1974: 169), 'Taxation of earnings from
labour is on a par with forced labour' and it is by no means clear that claims to
welfare rights override rights to property. Conflicting claims have to be
reconciled in the light of justice and not with reference to the worthwhileness
of what is being claimed as a right.

Such a philosophy is essentially a defence of self-interest against State
interests and as such it was an important piece of intellectual equipment in the
seventeenth century. It continues to be important, but it conflicts with other
points of view on both the left and the right which emphasize society and the
State as being of greater importance than the individuals who comprise them.

John Locke's contribution

In order to understand more recent deontological theory, it might help if we consider some of its origins and John Locke is an obvious starting point.

Locke's thought is set within a framework of 'natural law' which is unfamiliar to most present-day readers, but the problems with which he deals are familiar ones. In establishing a defence against an absolute monarchy, Locke tries to establish the supremacy of individuals each of whom has a fundamental natural-law right to existence. Following from this, they have additional supporting rights to those possessions which are necessary to secure their existence and a right to choose on matters which affect their individuality.

Locke's starting point is a *prima facie* case against absolute governments and he postulates a minimal role for the State or Commonwealth. For Locke, the State is an institution for the protection of individuals. It is not and does not have, in the Hegelian sense, an entity with a prior existence to which individuals owe an overriding obligation.

In his *Letter on Toleration,* Locke (1689 and 1956: 128) states that 'The Commonwealth seems to me to be a society of men constituted only for the procuring, preserving and advancing of their own civil interests'. These interests are defined as 'liberty, health and indolency of body; and the provision of outward things such as money, lands, houses, furniture and the like'. Furthermore: 'It is the duty of the civil magistrate, by the impartial execution of equal laws, to secure unto all people in general and every one of his subjects in particular, the just possession of these things belonging to this life'.

In effect, Locke has committed himself to a political platform which has to be theoretically justified. His justification is derived initially from Biblical texts, but the underlying principles, which are to be seen as *a priori*, do not necessarily depend upon political authority. What Locke tries to demonstrate is the existence of 'rights' possessed by all individuals which are antecedent to the establishment of society. These rights are the product of social contracts agreed by individuals of equal status.

The idea of antecedent natural rights requires Locke (1689 and 1956: 4) to postulate a natural state of man prior to any form of social organisation. He claims that men are in a 'state of perfect freedom to order their actions and dispose of their possessions and persons as they think fit within the bounds of the law of nature, without asking leave or depending upon the will of any other man'. Locke also considers it 'reasonable and just' to be allowed to destroy that which threatens an individual with destruction.

It might be objected that, in claiming antecedent rights, Locke is already drawing upon social concepts and that 'rights', 'freedom' and 'property' presuppose the existence of rules which define and protect them. We might say that a wild animal has a right to 'kill' but to talk in terms of property rights in such contexts is to use the terms metaphorically.

In order to escape from such objections, Locke (1689 and 1956: 14) is obliged to introduce the idea of the right to self-preservation based on God's law. We are deemed to possess 'natural reason' as a gift from God which 'tells us that men being born have a right to their preservation and consequently to meat and drink and such other things as nature affords for their subsistence'. We have therefore 'a property' in our own person and in those things necessary to our preservation. Furthermore, we have a duty to God to preserve ourselves.

These are no more than *a priori* assumptions but they are logically necessary in support of Locke's political position. If it is not accepted as a starting point that all individuals are worthy of preservation then further claims about their welfare become irrelevant because there is no basis on which to justify them.

It should be noted that Locke has introduced a strongly normative element into his case in the concept of 'property'. The term includes both material possession and health and liberty. The right to self-preservation is thereby extended to cover not merely the right to exist but the right to exist in a particular qualitative sense for which material possessions and other forms of property are necessary. It is not even enough to be provided with such things. Ownership must be vested in them. As society becomes more sophisticated and things like education are added to what is deemed necessary for a qualitative or normative view of 'existence' it is easy to see how they are then assimilated into the list of things to which we are said to have a right. Politically speaking, therefore, Locke has cleverly secured his position.

Because Locke's State is concerned only with the protection of individuals and the maintenance of justice, it is not necessary for him to consider any other possible ends or purposes. Each individual is free to choose his own 'good life' and it is in no way incumbent upon the State to provide for people beyond a framework of 'justice'. For the State to play any part in defining social policy would be regarded as an infringement of individual liberty; therefore the powers of government must be contained within very strict limits.

The idea of a 'minimal State' has been reviewed and restated in recent years by Richard Nozick in his book *Anarchy, State and Utopia* (1974). It has attracted a good deal of attention, partly because of the rigour of the argument presented, and also because it is so much in tune with present-day political thinking.

What is significant about such views, and it is central to the deontological philosophy, is that the absence of governmental influence in social policy is regarded as a virtue which overrides considerations of general welfare. It is regarded as more important that individual freedom should be extended and maintained even though this might lead to reductions in publicly provided welfare services, including education. The furtherance of 'the good' is seen as a personal rather than a collective concern, and the defence of 'rights' is more important, than, say, the amelioration of poverty.

Rawls and Nozick

Although each of these writers arrives at different political conclusions, they both start from similar philosophical presuppositions about the 'rights-based' ethic. Both writers draw upon the Kantian view that as 'centres of consciousness' each person should be regarded as an end and never as a means. We can never meaningfully ask 'for what purpose should a person be allowed to choose?' or 'why is self-development important?' These are ends deemed to be self-evidently worthwhile.

The relevance of this to liberal adult education should be obvious because it too is defended as a worthwhile end which need not be justified by reference to instrumental purposes. On this view 'education' is good, not something which furthers the good.

For Nozick (1974: 93), as for Locke:

'. . . there is no *social entity* with a good to which individuals contribute. There are only individual people, different individual people, with their own individual lives. Using one of these people for the benefit of others, uses him and benefits the others . . . To use him in this way does not sufficiently respect and take account of the fact that he is a separate person, that his is the only life he has'.

This robust defence of the individual has to be reconciled with the fact that in most situations, an individual's decisions about his own life are likely to react upon the interests of other people. Locke in fact recognised this point and qualified an individual's right to possession and the fruits of his labour except in conditions where there is an abundance of resources. We can only claim an absolute right to possessions such as land 'where there is enough and as good left in common for others'. In most cases, we find ourselves in a competitive situation and it is there that the need for fairness and distributive justice arises. Constraints are then imposed in order to regulate competition and to resolve conflicts of interest. The theoretical problem is to provide a justification for the constraints upon individual actions which must themselves be arrived at in such a way that individual freedom is respected. What Rawls tries to do is to explain how the regulating principles of 'rights' and 'justice' can be arrived at and accepted by free agents. One possible solution would be the utilitarian one which assumes that the regulating principles would lead to the maximization of some general good such as 'happiness' or 'economic welfare'. Utilitarianism, however, deals in generalities and it is in principle possible to maximize the general good in such a way that some individuals are left worse off. The rich might have to be heavily taxed, for example, or some people might be denied important freedom in the interests of the common good.

On the deontological principle, however, the common good cannot be allowed to become the prime concern from which policy is derived. Personal autonomy and the right to choose are primary and it is 'the good' which must be compromised if need be. Therefore Rawls, as did Locke before him, resorts to the idea of a social contract to establish the State and the principles which will regulate it. But Rawls wished to succeed where Locke had failed.

In justifying his principles of 'rights' and 'justice', Locke had introduced the notion of a duty to preserve oneself derived from the premise that 'God should be obeyed'. That in effect was a conception of the 'good'. Rawls sought a stronger position which, as Sandel (1982: 2) puts it, requires that 'principles of justice are justified in such a way that does not depend on any particular vision of the good. To the contrary, given the independent status, the right constrains the good and sets its bounds'.

The basis of this view is in Kant's claim that any conception of the good will be a purely contingent matter arrived at in the light of various 'interests', and can never be universal. It would be wrong, therefore, to commit ourselves to a particular contingent end. The universal moral imperative is the idea of morality itself and our ability to be moral depends upon our status as autonomous agents. A necessary requirement for being autonomous is the absence of any constraints which affect our capacity for making rational judgements. Kant therefore postulates 'selves' as centres of consciousness and reason, which are prior to and independent of any interests or attributes which we happen to have as a contingent fact. The individual is conceived as the irreducible 'I', who chooses in a way analogous with Descartes' 'self' which thinks and has experiences but which is not itself the object of an experience. This is a very rarefied conception of the 'self' but Rawls commits himself to a similar view.

In arriving at his version of the social contract, Rawls (1972: 11) asks us 'to imagine that those who engage together in social cooperation choose together in one joint act, the principles which are to assign basic rights and duties . . . Men are to decide in advance how they are to regulate their claims against one another'. The choices made must be wholly rational but in Rawls' view (1972: 17-18):

'A problem of rational decision has a definite answer only if we know the beliefs and interests of the parties, their relation with respect to one another, the alternatives between which they are to choose, the procedures whereby they make up their minds, and so on'.

In real life, we cannot know all the beliefs and interests of all the parties and even if we did know, there is likely to be gross inequality between individuals, and their interests and beliefs are likely to conflict. Therefore, in order that we might be sure that any social contract arrived at is rationally justified and therefore the 'correct' choice, we must be sure about the beliefs and interests of the parties to the decision. Moreover, there must be equality and a lack of contradiction between the various beliefs and interests, otherwise no determinate solution can be arrived at.

Rawls therefore introduces a set of simplifying assumptions and conditions which specify an 'original position' logically equivalent to Locke's 'state of nature'.

The 'original position' is called the 'veil of ignorance'. Behind this veil the participants are unaware of any interests, beliefs or other non-rational (that is to say 'contingent') influences which would cloud their judgement. Their only awareness is of themselves and they have no knowledge of how the various alternatives will affect their own particular case once they emerge from behind the veil.

Rawls (1972: 11-12) has set up a theoretical procedure which is intended to ensure that a wholly rational choice will emerge based upon no conception of 'the good', beyond 'the principles that free and rational persons concerned to further their own interest would accept in an initial position of equality. No one can 'favour his particular condition'.

What emerges and what Rawls (1972: 124) intends should emerge, is the idea of 'justice and fairness' and a system of 'rights' based on two main principles of justice:

(a)   the principle of greatest equal liberty;
(b)   (i) the principle of (fair) equality of opportunity;
          (ii) the difference principle.

The difference principle is equivalent to Locke's qualification that one can only hold possessions if 'as much and as good is left to other men'. Rawls justifies any possible inequality in distribution if, and only if, the inequality makes the worst off individual better off than he otherwise would have been.

Capital accumulation in the hands of a minority is justified, for example, if the resulting output is higher than under any other distribution of capital and if even the poorest gets goods at a lower price.

Taken together, principles (a), (b) (i) and (b) (ii) establish 'justice' as the first virtue of institutions, as truth is of systems of thought (Rawls 1972:3), and justice alone can guarantee the defence of each individual's self-interest.

As Sandel (1982: 15-16) observes:
' justice is not merely an important value to be weighed and considered as the occasion requires but rather the *means* by which values are weighed and

assessed. We need not ask whether a society or a social policy is "good" but only whether it is "just"'.

Deontological liberalism establishes the 'right', i.e. what is 'just', as prior to and independent of 'the good'. It is concerned only with the procedures for the regulation of society and not at all with substantive issues which might be deemed to have a bearing on 'the good life', or what is regarded as worthwhile. Such things as public libraries, theatres, education, health services and so on may be provided only if to do so is consistent with justice and not because they are in some sense thought to be 'good'.

The concept of 'justice' also presupposes the concept of 'truth' because one cannot make judgements about particular cases without being sure of the facts of the case. These two concepts are therefore central regulators and they link social and political philosophy with epistemology, each of which has a strongly individualistic orientation. In the Cartesian tradition, individual self-consciousness is the basis of knowledge and rational empiricism depends upon the perceptions of individuals tested against the perceptions of other people. The concept of 'justice' is now brought into the liberal tradition in order to defend the integrity of the individual.

The 'self' is one individual in a 'plurality of individuals' to use Sandel's phrase, and is the most important concept as the source of knowledge and reason. 'Justice' is necessary as the ethical and legal concept to protect individuals *because* they are the source of reason and are seen as ends which require no further justification. Their rights to liberty should not be overridden in the interests of 'society as a whole' because to the deontologist this phrase is a meaningless fiction. What the Rawlsian argument ignores is that the rarefied concept of the 'self' is itself a fiction, and the deontological case is based on claims about the status of individuals rather than on their ontological basis. The self-conscious centre of reason is a philosopher's invention and in common usage we tend to define 'persons' as 'individuals' in terms of describable attributes. It is these which give persons their individuality and enables us to distinguish between them. Disembodied 'selves' possess no distinguishing features and are thus deprived of individuality in any meaningful sense. Deontological theory removes the content from that which it sets out to protect. Rawls' individuals are reduced to the 'Archimedean points' which he says are required to assess the social system (1972: 261).

The deontological philosophy is intended to provide a liberating vision and its political purpose is to provide a formulation for claims to 'liberty'. What it is in danger of doing in practice is to establish a climate in which a jealous concern for 'rights' clouds all vision of what a society might become, and there are signs that this is happening in Western societies. On all sides, the right to choose appears to be regarded as more important than what is chosen. This view is manifest in politics and also the arts where traditions and standards seem to be discarded in favour of individual expression, without too much concern for the worthwhileness of what is expressed.

This brings us back to adult education where the influence of deontological liberalism may be seen in 'andragogical theory'. 'Learning', which is an undifferentiated concept, has tended to emerge in preference to the value-based and normative concept of 'education'. It is regarded as more important that individuals should learn what they choose, than that they should learn something important and worthwhile. The refusal to make judgements between different kinds and different areas of learning is found even in official documents such as the ACACE Report on *Continuing Education: from Policies to Practice*. All learning might be of equal value if personal choice is the major criterion but it should be asked whether this view is helping to trivialize adult education. Do we need a philosophy which helps us to identify what is most worthwhile and to establish priorities in education?

Our liberalism could be a disintegrating philosophy instead of a liberating one. The 'self' can also be viewed as a 'social self', a part of a whole, and the unity of society rather than the Rawlsian unity of the self might well be reasserted in order to counteract disintegrating tendencies.

Deontological liberalism has deep roots, but as a tradition it produces societies which no longer debate or seek 'the good'. It is a philosophy suited to a society which has no vision. Its clearest manifestation is in a free-enterprise monetary economy. It is less important to ask *what* is being produced than to ask how much and of what monetary value is being produced. Profit and cost efficiency is what matters and these concepts are the economic equivalents of 'rights' and 'justice'. They are impersonal criteria which enable us to concentrate on processes and to avoid the value questions about what is good. Monetary values are the criteria by which all subsequent values are judged and they must not be overridden by considerations of what is worthwhile. Monetary values *define* worthwhileness.

It may be worth asking ourselves whether liberal adult educators have exacerbated the situation by apparently avoiding educational value questions. It is fashionable to say that adult education is about *process* not content. This is eminently a deontological view. Is it an adequate one? Are we trying to lead a culture into losing its way or are we following in a society which has lost its way? These are big questions and they point to a current lack of critical awareness at a number of points. Can we go on without some conception of purpose and what is worthwhile? Such a question should be a challenge to adult education. Is our liberalism in the end too empty of content and concerned only with processes? If so, should we try to redefine our philosophy in a more meaningful way which respects individuals but defines them as part of a group and not independently of it?

3

Liberal education, rule governed behaviour and legal philosophy

Introduction

In my article on 'Deontological liberalism: the political philosophy of liberal adult education' (Lawson, 1985), I drew attention to the emphasis in that 'philosophy' upon free and rational choice and upon the notions of 'justice' and 'rights' as regulators of choice. These notions are all based upon the ideas of 'rules' and 'principles', and rational behaviour is essentially 'rule governed' in some sense. To behave rationally is to behave intentionally and in ways which are consistent with the intention. It is expected that there shall be logical connections between ends and means and that logically valid procedures shall be followed in arriving at decisions. Courses of action will be judged according to logical criteria.

The exact nature of the rules which are expected to be followed in rational behaviour might be open to debate, but rules *per se* are a necessary feature. The idea of behaviour which is governed by rules might seem to contradict the ideal of 'free choice' or 'rational autonomy', the achievement of which is a frequently expressed aim in liberal education. Rules are suggestive of constraint and imposition and can be regarded as inimical to the ideas of freedom and autonomy.

Nevertheless, the concept of liberal education draws heavily upon the idea of disciplined thinking which is implicit in the whole idea of a knowledge-based curriculum and upon academic disciplines.

Unless the idea of 'rational autonomy' is to be seen as hopelessly contradictory as an aim in liberal education, a clearer understanding of the nature and place of 'rules' in our thinking seems to be necessary and this article explores some aspects of the notion of 'rule governed behaviour'. It suggests that such behaviour is not inconsistent with the idea of 'free' or 'autonomous' behaviour and is actually a precondition for it.

Many of the ideas and arguments to be presented are drawn from legal philosophy, and law is seen as a model of a system of rules in an attempt to demonstrate the theory of rules or the quasi legal philosophy implicit in the concept of liberal education.

In addition to the idea of 'rules' implicit in the concept of 'law', there are also the ideas of 'authority' and 'objectivity' and it is the former which seems likely to provoke hostility to the idea of 'rule governance' in education, because education then seems to be an instrument of social control rather than a vehicle for freedom. It can of course become oppressive if used to express the ideology and aims of a particular power group, but it is the purpose of the idea of 'objectivity' and the related idea of 'justice' to counter this possibility.

Authority in education

In recent years, R S Peters has introduced the idea of 'authority' into educational philosophy, together with the idea of 'rule governed behaviour'. In *Ethics and Education* (1966) it is asserted that the two ideas are 'inseparably connected'. It is also suggested that 'Authority . . . presupposes some sort of normative order that has to be promulgated, maintained and perpetuated . . . There are procedural rules which give [some] people the right to decide, promulgate, judge, order and pronounce' (Peters, 1966: 238).

Such language, as Peters rightly points out, ' . . . has its natural home in legal systems, armies and religious communities' (Peters, 1966: 239). For the educator a critical question is whether such language can be translated into open democratic communities where everyone has some right to 'decide, promulgate and judge'.

'Authority' language presupposes either a corresponding power which makes enforcement possible, or a sense of commitment because of the inherent merit or rightness of whatever is decided or promulgated. In education, as in law, power and the threat of sanctions does reside in institutions and individual teachers, but the liberal ideal is based upon the acceptance of knowledge based upon 'truth telling' and objectivity. There are standards by which to judge decisions, arguments and performance, which are themselves accepted as worth while and beyond the mere opinion of any single individual. This is part of what is meant by 'objectivity' and both liberalism and rationality rest on a commitment to these ideas.

At each stage in the decision we are pushed back to the idea of 'procedures' and criteria for judging the particular procedures to be followed when acquiring and formulating knowledge, constructing and presenting arguments or producing artefacts. There need not be a single criterion or a single set of criteria for what constitutes a good argument, a substantiated knowledge claim or a well-designed and constructed artefact. It is necessary, however, that some criteria can be alluded to in defence or justification of a procedure and its outcome. Thus, impersonal frames of reference are provided and the autonomy which they are intended to guarantee has to be understood in a rather special sense. We are freed from the non-rational dictates of others and we can test or judge our own responses against an objective reference point. On both counts, therefore, we are insulated against emotion, self-interest and instinct. Behind such thinking, however, there is a presumption in favour of the possibility of a rational 'will.' Truth and truth telling are twin pillars of the theological edifice analogous to fairness, justice and rights in the political and legal domain.

In securing one kind of freedom and autonomy, it might be argued that we simply place ourselves under the yoke of rationality and the idea of governance by rules. One can ask, therefore, why we should commit ourselves to such principles. Is there a categorical imperative which demands such commitment or do we accept on some kind of pragmatic utilitarian grounds? R S Peters and others seem to argue, however, that we are transcendentally committed to such notions as 'truth' and 'rationality' in the very act of trying to establish in various contexts whether we are doing the correct thing or saying the right thing. We are thereby in effect committing ourselves to linking means and ends. Discussion of these issues is, however, beyond the scope of this article and they have been discussed elsewhere (see, for example, Beck, 1971). It is proposed therefore, to consider the nature and implications of the idea of 'rules' and 'rule governed behaviour' in a little more detail in order to assess what it is that we are being committed to.

Rules and laws

Although the concept of 'law' cannot be explicated exhaustively in terms of 'rules' (see Dworkin, 1977), there is a sense in which laws can be regarded as special kinds of rules, 'used by the community directly or indirectly for the purpose of determining which behaviour will be punished or coerced by the public power' (Dworkin, 1977: 38). On the other hand, there are laws which govern the relationships between people by defining property rights, etc., and which regulate commercial dealings. They are not necessarily backed by threats of punishment. We also speak of having legal *obligations* which suggests that (some) laws make moral demands upon us quite apart from any idea of coercion. The analysis of the concept of 'obligation' and the relationship between law and morality is a major issue in the philosophy of law.

What is known as the 'positivist' view of law separates 'law' from morality and it is assumed that laws have to be obeyed, even though they might be morally outrageous. The source of obligation has to be sought elsewhere than in morality and abstract conceptions of 'justice' and 'rights'. To the positivist, it is necessary only that laws are *valid* in the sense that they have been formulated according to legally and constitutionally correct procedures. In other words, if laws are correctly formulated rules, there is an obligation to obey them *because* they are *rules* and not because they are (morally) *good* rules.

A non-legal analogy would be the rules of a private club with its own constitution. No doubt its rules have to conform in some respects with prevailing legal requirements but within these limits, rules are binding upon members of the club, whatever an individual member might think of them, provided that the club's constitution and traditional procedures had been observed when the rules were drawn up, proposed and adopted. If the rules are unacceptable to a member, there is no alternative but to resign.

The point to be made is that the force of rules, on this view, derives from criteria of procedural correctness. What a particular rule contingently specifies is of no concern at this stage of the argument which rests on the binding force of rules or laws as they *happen* to be, rather than on broader considerations as they *ought* to be. In positivist eyes, law is not normative but pragmatic.

In educational terms the analogy is between 'normative' and 'descriptive' concepts of education. The former entails a value-based ideal of education as it ought to be whereas the latter takes education as it is in concrete situations.

Both in law and in education there is room for argument about the application of terms because to say of something that it is an example of 'education' is to make certain assumptions about the conditions appropriate to the use of the term 'education'. Some minimum defining characteristics of education have to be assumed in order to give the word use and meaning. The boundary between 'normative' and 'descriptive' uses of the term 'education', therefore, become blurred. Similarly, we might ask whether laws are only a particular kind of rule which happens to be backed by power or whether their authority derives in part from a normative element contained within the definition of 'law'. Neither education nor law seems to be without a normative component in this minimal sense and they are employed in socio-political contexts in which values are held or presupposed, and in which people hold expectations and intentions to which concepts such as education give support. Such concepts cannot be wholly detached from their social frames of reference.

In the hands of writers such as R S Peters, the concept of 'education' is primarily seen as a normative concept which should be seen from ' . . . inside a form of life' and which ' . . . is inseparable from talk of what is worth while' (Peters, 1967:5). The form of life is, as we have noted, one which is 'rule governed' and, therefore, rational.

If positivist theories of law emphasize the rule-like aspects of law and the procedures by which laws are made a source of definitions of law, and as a source of legal obligation, then a rule governed form of life is also presupposed. To that extent, therefore, a normative dimension seems to be implied. When thinkers such as Bentham and Austin declare the separation of law and morality as absolute, they are committing themselves to the rule of law *per se* and to the 'rule of rules'. Rules are their own justification because the form of life which engenders such thinking is one which by the actions of its adherents displays a logical dependence upon 'rationality' conceived as being rule governed and rule following. There is circularity in the arguments but 'rules' are central to it, and commitment to rules is a categorical imperative.

Law, morals and the rule of law

In order to elevate the 'rule of law' or 'rule of rules' to the position of an imperative, it is necessary to maintain a rigorous distinction between law and morality. Too sharp a distinction has its dangers, however, and the acceptance of some Nazi laws by members of the German legal profession is a case in point. Hart has described how some German positivists recognised the dangers and Gustav Radbruch consequently rejected 'law as law' (*Gesetz als Gesetz*) because of the horrors to which it led (see Hart, 1977: 30-31). This is one kind of danger. Another is manifest in such examples as the British reaction to the Argentinian occupation of the Falklands, which was condemned as a violation of the rule of law. If this principle is held at any cost whatsoever, the consequence is open violence in order to achieve what international law has failed to achieve. In extreme conditions, therefore, the rule of law is paradoxically put aside in defence of the rule of law. On the whole, experience suggests that nations do not actually go to war on grounds of principle but in defence of substantive interests and this suggests that in practice there are limits to the acceptance of the rule of law and for the moment this is the point that I wish to make.

There also appear to be limits to the idea of 'law' as a special kind of rule enforceable by power and threat of punishment. This limit appears when we try to argue that laws impose some kind of obligation, not because there is a sanction behind them which can be imposed upon offenders, but because they are *good* laws. They embody political, social and moral principles and they are intended as regulators of 'the good life'. It is not sufficient for a law to satisfy utilitarian ends. They must also be justifiable ends and what is a justifiable end is very much open to debate.

Dworkin makes the point that when a law is regarded purely as a rule, a particular law specifies the 'conditions that make its application necessary' (Dworkin, 1977:47). Thus, if a law specifies that certain kinds of contract are not valid unless they have three signatures, then a document of the specified type has to be ruled invalid if only two signatures are appended. The rule must be applied to all cases which fit its particular conditions. In contrast to this, Dworkin argues that principles embodied in law act in effect as ethical guidelines, thus, 'A principle like "no man may profit from his own wrong" does not even purport to set out conditions that make its applications necessary. Rather it states a reason that argues in one direction' (Dworkin, 1977: 47). Such principles carry *weight* or importance. They are taken into account and they *influence* legal decisions but they are not logically necessary conditions, and in this respect principles add to laws, a dimension that is not possessed by mere 'rules'. When 'two rules conflict, one of them cannot be a valid rule' (Dworkin, 1977: 48) in those particular circumstances. Conflicting principles on the other hand might each apply to a given case but in varying degrees and their relative weight has to be judged or assessed. The significance of this is that legal decisions are not only a matter of strict logical entailment arrived at by the application of logical techniques mechanically applied. A computer could make such decisions but it cannot add the extra-logical dimension of judgement on which assessments of the weight of principles depend. Such assessments do not seem to depend entirely upon the application of *further* rules. Certain procedures, such as consideration of precedents, might be followed, but the final decision is a 'leap in the dark' not strictly entailed by rules of logic. In this respect, legal judgements are not unlike decisions in most spheres of activity. A decision is not a logical conclusion drawn from valid deductions. There is a sense in which decisions are 'acts of faith', although they might be based on reasons of some kind. What makes them decisions and not deductions is the fact that they go beyond the dictates of rules into an area where there are no further rules. Rule governed behaviour, therefore, carries with it a dimension which is not in the strict sense governed by rules.

There are other ways in which law appears to go beyond being a strictly rule invoking and rule governed domain, and this may be illustrated by reference to what have been called 'problems of the penumbra'. H L A Hart notes on this point:

> ' . . . that when Bentham and Austin insisted on the distinction between law as it is and law as it ought to be, they had in mind *particular* laws, the meanings of which were clear and not in dispute' (Hart, 1977: 177).

Many laws seem to be not of this kind and they are ambiguous as to meaning and uncertain in their precise application. They require interpretation by Courts. Hart therefore says:

> 'We may call the problems which arise outside the hard core of standard instances or settled meanings, "problems of the penumbra"; they are always with us, whether in relation to such trivial things as the regulation of the use of the public park or in relation to the multidimensional generalities of a constitution. If a penumbra of uncertainty must surround all legal rules,

then their application to specific cases cannot be a matter of logical deduction, and so deductive reasoning ... cannot serve as a model for what judges, or indeed anyone should do in bringing particular cases under general rules' (Hart, 1977: 23).

Among other things, problems of the penumbra involve questions of definition as when considering whether, for the purposes of particular laws, an aeroplane is or is not a 'vehicle'. Another example might be the question of whether a hovercraft is subject to the laws governing aerial navigation or the rules of the sea. Such issues are not unique to law but are also commonplace in academic discussions where definitions can be crucial, and categorial distinctions are often unclear.

Views on such matters can be disputed, and once the idea of contestability is introduced into law or any other area governed by rules, we are taken beyond the point at which it can be claimed that rules are followed or accepted simply because they are rules. In arriving at agreement on definitions and decisions upon areas of application of particular rules, we draw upon principles, appropriateness and fitness of purpose in the light of what we are trying to achieve and what we believe ought to be achieved. Each agreement and each decision has to be seen and understood in a context of purposes, values, and so on.

In all this, we are operating at a number of levels, in so far as rules are concerned, and a distinction drawn up by Hart and referred to by Dworkin outlines a point made earlier about the importance of procedures in validating rules. Hart refers to 'primary' rules which either grant rights or impose obligations. Behind these are the secondary rules which specify how and by whom 'primary rules may be formed, recognised, modified, or extinguished' (Dworkin, 1977: 40). Primary rules are, therefore, open to scrutiny in terms of their genesis and antecedents. At each stage, however, the primary rules can be subjected to similar processes of examination and this is precisely what happens within academic disciplines in which methodology and basic principles are themselves important and subject to constant review and revision.

Conclusion

If rules are approached in the manner suggested, the whole idea of being rule governed becomes less restricting and less intimidating. The concept of a 'rule governed form of life' may be seen as very open textured, and it is procedural rather than substantive. Its procedures in turn are open to revision and rather than being a constraint, rules are enabling; they need not be final.

An educational curriculum consistent with such views is implicit in the concept of liberal education and it seems to be no accident that the liberal tradition has generated critiques of its own procedures. I refer here to the debates about relativism in epistemology, the questioning of knowledge-generating procedures, the attention drawn to the importance of power structures in the formulation and dissemination of knowledge and so on. That such debates have received attention in recent years is an encouraging sign. Nevertheless, it has to be borne in mind that in questioning particular rules and procedures, we are still committing ourselves to further rules and procedures and it seems to be an open question whether we can or should ever arrive at a permanent definitive situation.

Liberal education, therefore, should be seen as entailing a commitment to the idea of procedures of some kind in our thinking, but not necessarily to a particular substantive set of procedures. There is an assumption that we also commit ourselves to an infinitely extendable appraisal and modification of our procedures and the rules used to define and substantiate knowledge claims. Conformity to rules of *some* kind is required if we are to retain the twin concepts of 'rationality' and 'knowledge', and the latter ceases to have meaning without the apparatus of rules and agreed 'good reasons' behind knowledge claims. A claim that 'x' is the case becomes a valid claim only when its genesis is known. We claim typically that 'we have checked the evidence' for the claim, but what counts as evidence in a particular field of knowledge, and what counts as an appropriate set of tests of the evidence can change over a period of time. The process of change in turn is tested against procedural criteria. To some extent, these criteria are enshrined in institutional arrangements and what is regarded as a good criterion by which to judge, and what is a relevant question to ask, will no doubt be influenced by the avowed purposes of institutions (such as universities) and the intentions of people with them. But we can then go on to assess these purposes and intentions as another phase in our rational procedure. For the academic, the questions asked about methods used to produce and validate knowledge, will be formulated in a context in which a high valuation is placed upon the collection of knowledge as an end. The ongoing assessment of the rules of enquiry presupposes the value of the enquiry.

For those in government and in industry, enquiry is related to more pragmatic ends such as the provision of welfare services and material wealth on the one hand, or the establishment and maintenance of power on the other. These ends are themselves in need of evaluation and assessment and society requires criteria for judging what count as 'good' or worthwhile ends: we are brought once again to the criteria by which these judgments are made and the procedures by which the criteria are arrived at. The issues are partly logical, they are partly ethical and they are also political because we are concerned with the 'rationality' of judgement about ends and means, their morality, and the institutional frameworks and political processes within which the whole system operates.

We are in all this expressing a view about the nature of society, and, properly understood, 'rule governance' is a precondition of a particular 'liberal' view of society, with which the idea of liberal education is intimately connected. It might be seen as an excessively idealistic view of society and of education. It also contains its own flaw within it in that a process of ongoing questioning and reassessment of all goals, rules and procedures produces no resting place or point of permanence on which lasting agreement might be reached. It is this feature which produces the philosophy of individualism which also underlines liberalism and which leads many to say that no person can judge what is good for another. In claiming the right to say and do our 'own thing', however, the liberal tradition also carries with it a duty to submit our personal decisions to judgement according to rules and procedures. We can, therefore, see 'rules' as a control but these rules also permit us to enjoy the conviction that our judgments and decisions are justifiable. Liberal education is a key element in that it is the vehicle by means of which we acquire the skills to operate within such a system. It is not an optional and dispensable extra.

4

From Citizen to Self

Introduction

This chapter is based upon the assumption that adult education is not free-standing and can only be studied within a broader cultural context which provides its values. In an earlier essay (Lawson, 1985), I explored connections between 'deontological' or 'rights-based' liberalism and liberal adult education, but a broader view is necessary in order to produce a more accurate picture. Other dimensions within the liberal tradition will be drawn upon because they, too, correlate with theory and practice in adult education.

Neither 'liberalism' nor 'liberal adult education' are simple concepts and they are not static. It is because they change, that the idea of a 'tradition' is introduced. It suggests dynamism in response to changing circumstances.

Alasdair MacIntyre (1988) has suggested that the original liberal project was seen by many as an attempt to escape from the contingency of tradition by 'appealing to genuinely tradition-independent norms'. The new norms were thought to be universal whereas they constituted a particular vision of an ideal political system. What emerged was another tradition with its own values which became definitive of and normative within the tradition. The new vision was *meant* to be *liberating* but it was also *constraining*, thus creating inherent tensions.

The subsequent history of liberalism might be seen in part as a series of attempts to remove the tension by slackening the normative requirements, but it will be argued that this is not an achievable goal. By reducing the number of defining characteristics, the tradition becomes less determinate, more ambiguous, and in the end dissolves. To be a tradition at all, recognisable limits are essential, although it does not follow that change is impossible. New norms may be introduced but these can change the tradition in ways that make it incompatible with its earlier manifestations. It ceases to be recognisable as the same tradition.

This seems to be happening, or to have happened already and it is now difficult to be precise about what is meant by 'liberalism' in either political or educational terms. It becomes necessary therefore to identify different strands and to attempt some form of classification. This will be done selectively within the confines of a single essay and no attempt is made to present a potted history. The selections are meant to be illustrative only, and where they are linked, the connections are in logical rather than in temporal sequence, even though this might make the argument somewhat disjointed. The author can see a pattern and it is hoped that readers will do so, too.

What might we mean by 'liberalism'?

In *A Matter of Principle*, Ronald Dworkin (1986: 181, 183) explores the hypothesis put forward by sceptics that politically speaking, 'there is no such thing as liberalism although his project suggests that there is'. We are in a similar position.

Dworkin continues:

'. . . before the Vietnam war, politicians who called themselves 'liberals' held certain *positions* that could be identified as a group. Liberals were for greater economic equality, for internationalism, for freedom of speech, for greater equality between races, for procedural protection of accused criminals . . . and for an aggressive use of central government power to achieve these goals'.

This last point might seem strange to those who regard *minimal* government as a liberal ideal. Minimal government is also a mark of modern conservatism, and it is this kind of ambiguity in practice which makes liberalism difficult to identify. But it clearly is not a prerogative of any one political party and in that sense it is politically neutral. Dworkin's list of 'causes' is given unity by a number of common *principles* which include 'equality', 'freedom' and 'justice', although he himself argues that 'the nerve of liberalism' is 'a certain concept of equality'.

Thomas Nagel (1982: 191) suggests that liberalism is:

'. . . the conjunction of two ideals . . . the first of which is individual liberty,' [and the second is a] 'democratic society controlled by its citizens'.

For him, liberty is a prime value and democracy is merely a mechanism which makes liberty possible. It does not necessarily follow that democracy entails minimal government and Nagel makes a minimalist conclusion dependent upon his particular definition of liberty. This he *defines* as ' . . . freedom from government interference with privacy, personal life and the exercise of individual inclinations'. Other definitions are possible.

J S Mill (1859 and 1962: 135) made a similar point in his *Essay on Liberty* although he allowed governments to intervene in private life in certain circumstances. Mill actually defines very narrowly the area of 'private space' and he makes his individuals sovereign only over their 'own body and mind' and an individual in his theory should *always* be prevented from doing harm to others. His utilitarianism also takes him beyond this point, and despite saying that no one should be forced to act for their *own* good, he claimed that '. . . there are many positive acts for the benefit of others which [an individual] may rightfully be *compelled* to perform' (1859 and 1962: 136).

Mill's stance, in effect, makes the good of others at least as important as a concern for privacy and self-interest and by holding these two points in a finely balanced tension, he can say, without contradiction, that we may be *required* to perform 'acts of beneficence' (1859 and 1962: 131).

This brings us back to Dworkin's claim about the importance of 'equality' which is implicit in Mill's argument about the good of others and the obligation to be beneficent. Nagel (1982: 191) also introduces the idea of equality when he says that, in order to make his other principles operative, it is necessary that there should be no 'excessive . . . inequalities of political and economic power and social position'.

We can see in this discussion how various principles interrelate in a systematic way and in doing so become normative, by definition. Moreover, none of the principles are brought in from other systems. They are already *liberal* principles and liberal values and their justification is implicit within the system. They are already justified because they *are* liberal principles; they are constitutive of liberalism. They provide the basis for its rules, define the 'game' as it has evolved, and have no force beyond it.

This brings out a further point, namely that the liberal vision of politics is rule-based. It is a rational form of politics in the sense that it relates ideas in a logical sequence. Its inherent rationality is the reference point for guiding and judging action. Mill (1859 and 1962: 136) reinforces this view when he says that:

> '. . . liberty as a principle has no application to any state of things anterior to the time when mankind has become capable of being improved by free and equal *discussion*. Until that time, there is nothing but implicit obedience . . .'

This emphasis on discussion as a necessary condition for achieving liberty amounts to an implicit injunction on the use of force for that end, although that is not Mill's purpose. His stress on discussion arises from a belief that 'individuality' is expressible only through an ability 'to form opinions' and 'to express them without reserve' (1859 and 1962: 184).   Individuality is therefore being defined in terms of the ability to discuss in order that 'liberty' may then be defined as 'freedom to discuss'. Both 'liberty' and 'discussion' help to define 'individuality' which would otherwise have no place in Mill's vocabulary. For him, 'liberty' cannot be defined any other way. Not even the *nature* of our opinion counts. It is sufficient that we have opinions of *some* kind and can express them.

We might summarise this brief discussion in the following terms:

1)   Liberalism represents a strongly moral approach to politics. Dworkin's list of 'causes' consists of goals which *ought* to be realised. They are not simply 'causes' which would be politically *expedient*, although they might additionally have utilitarian purpose.

2)   The causes cited are 'worthy' because they embody principles such as 'freedom' and 'equality' which are accepted as good justificatory reasons for taking action. These principles are simultaneously *concepts* and goals.

3)   There is a rational approach to politics based upon a rationality of seeking definable 'goods' rather than a naked struggle for power as an end. The goal is to control and define power, but by rational means as a normative principle.

4)   The concept of individuality is primary for several reasons:
        a) individuals provide the starting point of all thought and action.
        b) they are also deemed to be the end point or purpose of action.

5)   There is concern not only for self-interest but also the interests and welfare of others. There is a concern for responsibilities and duties, as well as rights.

Nevertheless this represents only one strand of liberalism within the broader tradition, because it emphasises the welfare of others, and is concerned with duties as well as rights. We might designate it by using Mill's own term, 'beneficence' to describe it as 'beneficent liberalism'; it might equally be called 'classical liberalism'.

We turn now to a review of some of the historical roots of this strand before considering others within the tradition. In doing so, I wish to draw particular attention to two major developments. The first is the changing perception of the nature of individuality and its role in political thought. The second, which is a consequence of the first, is the shift away from the idea of a public good towards the idea of private good. A third might be added as a gloss on each of these, and that is the narrowing of definitions of social relationships which weakens the values of 'community' implicit in the 'classical' strand.

Historical roots

We begin conventionally with Athenian democracy as it appeared towards the end of the fifth century BC. The account given is based substantially on a relatively new study by Cynthia Farrar (1989), who stresses the importance of concrete political issues as determinants of political theory.

Athenian democracy developed in a situation in which States were already established and what we would call problems of 'international relations' were a cause for concern. Fear of domination by another State was the most urgent problem and one especially important aspect was the fear of slavery, which conquest would bring if Athens lost her sovereignty. This is an especially important point because out of it developed the Athenian concept of negative freedom. It was simply 'freedom from slavery', and this concept had a profound effect upon Athenian thought and practice concerning internal government of the City State.

A strong government was obviously essential in order to maintain this freedom and effective control of social order was an important prerequisite for this end. The fear of slavery, that is to say, a loss of freedom in a very practical sense, provided a social bond which united private interests with the public interest. Individual freedom in the sense in which it was then understood, was dependent upon State sovereignty which, in turn, was recognised as being dependent upon the support of its citizens. This sense of mutual support was thus expressed in the institution of democratic government as an enabling mechanism, not a 'good', except to the extent that it fulfils a utilitarian purpose in securing commitment to political decisions. In fact, by the time of Plato, who was an anti-democrat, the idea of democracy was in disrepute.

On the back, as it were, of this very practical view of democracy a total view of social and political life was developing. From an internal point of view, 'the Athenians', as Farrar (1989: 7) puts it:

'did not construe the good to be secured politically in terms of direct material advantage. Political life expressed a shared, ordered self-understanding, not a mere struggle for power'.

These were quite sophisticated political ideals which were normative for an Athenian for whom:

' ... political status, the status of the citizen both marked and shaped man's identification with those aspects of human nature that made possible a reconciliation of personal aims and social order'.

This, Farrar (1989: 1) regards as a 'striking vision' of political principles. We may also see it as introducing the moral element into political life. Good citizenship became a moral imperative accepted voluntarily, but the idea of voluntarism depended in turn upon the ideal of citizens as 'autonomoi'; they had to be autonomous choosers in order to be deemed responsible for actions. Thus principle became interwoven with principle and what began as a limited concept of freedom developed into a set of ideas fundamental to the Athenian system. Abstract ideas and theory became a part of politics and social life in 'a dynamic synthesis of the concrete and the reflective'. But the process of development was piecemeal and as Farrar wryly comments, 'democracy was cobbled together' (1989: 1). It did not arrive as a ready-made dream but as a result of communal effort and, as H D F Kitto (1964: 11) expresses it:

> ' . . . the city-state was the means by which the Greeks consciously strove to make life, both of the community and of the individual, more excellent than it was before. [What began as] . . . a local association for common security, became the focus of man's moral, intellectual, aesthetic, social and practical life, developing and enriching these in a way in which no form of society had done before or has done since'.

It must of course be recognised that the citizens of Athens did not comprise the whole of its population because they were supported by a substratum of slaves and foreigners who had no part in political life. Citizenship was attained by birth and as G H Sabine (1949: 19) puts it: 'what citizenship entitled a man to was "membership" 'and this is a point which cannot be too heavily stressed when we look at the roots of modern liberalism. The concepts of individuality and autonomy were important but they were given expression in and through the sense of *membership* and it will be argued below that in more recent liberal thought, the emphasis has shifted excessively in favour of a socially disembodied form of individuality. We might, for want of a better term, call this 'postmodern' liberalism, or if preferred, we can use the clumsy term 'deontological liberalism'. It still falls within the same tradition but in many ways it is the opposite of Mill's 'beneficent' liberalism, which is more firmly rooted in classical thought. But new forms are a response to changing historical situations, and this should not surprise us if it is accepted that the liberal tradition is not a neutral philosophical tradition but one firmly rooted in practice.

Changing rationalities

In Athenian thought and in the writings of Mill we noted the stress placed upon the role of discussion as the basis of political life. This, when coupled with the idea of reflection, highlights the importance of 'reason' in liberal, democratic tradition. It was present at the beginning and has since become implicit as a constitutive element.

Thought and practice would cease to be liberal if reason was denied, because the liberal conception of mankind portrays men and women as rational beings, self-aware and articulate. Reason is made a precondition for 'autonomy'.

Philosophers such as Descartes (1637 and 1913) suggest that the capacity to think rationally is in some way 'natural' or innate, whereas the passage already quoted from Mill implies that the capacity developed historically. MacIntyre (1988) seems to share Mill's view when he says that intellectual enquiry, which presupposes rational thought, 'is part of the elaboration of a mode of social and moral life'. On this view 'rationality' does not depend upon abstract universal principles, it is something that is shared by those within a tradition within which particular rationalities evolved.

If this view is correct (and it is difficult to establish how any intellectual tradition can be established beyond all tradition, because we are speaking of human invention), the way is then open to the possibility of a multiplicity of rationalities and this, indeed, is the thrust of MacIntyre's argument.

There is a difficulty here, which MacIntyre (1988) admits, with the idea of logic as universal and he accepts areas of agreement in *some* standards for the regulation of argument. Nevertheless, within the liberal tradition there can be discerned differing views on what are acceptable as good reasons put forward in justification of particular actions and policies. Such variability is implied by the idea of a liberal tradition as distinct from a single liberal doctrine, because the latter would be unnecessarily restrictive and in itself a denial of liberalism. 'Tradition' both allows and requires recognition of difference, otherwise it ceases to be 'tradition' and this too is illustrative of tensions within liberalism because recognition of difference and plurality also becomes constitutive. The idea echoes Rousseau's famous call that we must 'force men to be free' and the paradox arises wherever 'freedom', however defined, becomes constitutive or normative for a tradition of thought.

I am aware of ambiguity in running together terms such as 'reason', 'rationality' and 'reflection', but for our present purpose these seem to be sufficiently cognate. We are already familiar with the idea of different forms of reasoning in the two examples 'inductive' and 'deductive' and Toulmin (1961) has explored different forms of reasoning in his book *Reason in Ethics*. The idea is also implicit in Wittgenstein's (1958) metaphor of 'language games' in which the 'logic' of a move and hence the meaning of words is definable only within a particular game or discourse.

One form of discourse is present in Athenian political thought and practice. For the Athenian citizen it was rational to identify and define personal goals in the light of the shared aim of preserving the independence and

and sovereignty of Athens. That a particular action was conducive to this end was a good and sufficient reason for recommending and taking that action. Such reasoning defined their political rationality.

Within this framework an idea such as 'autonomy' seemed *initially* to be pragmatically useful as a means of securing commitment although, as we have observed, there were constraints on what would be deemed 'good' or rational to choose. Choices had to be consistent with the value system as a whole and it is this sense of interrelatedness which makes it 'rational' within the root sense of that word, which is 'ratio' as 'the relationship of one thing to another'.

A different approach is evident in two other examples that have been used, namely Mill and Nagel. In his Essay, Mill (1859 and 1962: 126, 205) uncompromisingly spells out his project as being concerned with 'the nature and limits of the power which can be legitimately exercised by society over the individual'. The obverse of this is to define 'the rightful limit to the sovereignty of the individual'. Nagel (1982) expresses himself differently but he and Mill are concerned with the same issues, namely:

1)   the rights of individuals and the definition of their private space;
2)   the promotion of a society which serves the needs of individuals.

Here the implied rationality is not expressed in terms of defending the State by concerted effort. The first concern is to protect individual interests and this is the prime function of government. It is rational to do whatever is most conducive to *this* end. The first question must always be 'what promotes individual interests?' but, as Nagel (1982) observes, it is difficult to pursue the private and the public good simultaneously, hence Mill's claim that privacy may be invaded to do good to others. The political problem is to achieve some kind of unstable equilibrium in which the instability is the inevitable result of trying to define societal goals in terms of the sum of individual goods. There is no *independently defined public good* and this is why Mill has to introduce the idea of 'utility' as something to be maximised. We end up with a 'utilitarian' rationality which judges the validity of action on the basis of what produces the greatest total good. An action which achieves this is a rational action. It is Mill's solution to Nagel's problem, and it maintains the principle of 'beneficence'.

In John Locke (1698 and 1956), writing in the seventeenth century, a very different strand in the liberal tradition begins. Superficially, he is dealing with the same issues as Mill, in that he too is concerned with protecting the sovereignty of individuals. But two differences stand out. Locke is much more specific in his target, which is the containment of absolute monarchy, and Locke's individual is very differently conceived.

Starting from a natural law position he postulates an individual as having a natural law right to life and also rights to property or possessions, including the property of one's own body. The defence of property is the key to his rationality. Individuals, says Locke (1690 and 1956: 5), are 'in a state of perfect freedom to order their actions and dispose of their possessions and persons as they think fit within the bounds of nature, without asking leave'. Preservation of this freedom provides the foundation for a political platform to which his theory is directed.

His emphasis is not however on 'reason' and 'discussion' *per se.* He is concerned with a very much more circumscribed framework of rights enforcing law. The State, for Locke, becomes a regulator of contractual relationships between individuals and between individuals and the State. His rationality is procedural in the sense of being concerned with the application of rules, and the starting point is always of the form 'what rules govern this kind of case?' 'What are the procedures to be followed?'

Democracy is the preferred form of government, not in order to secure loyalty and commitment as in Athens, but as a mechanism for the diffusion of power. Locke is therefore consistent in his avowed aim of weakening, not strengthening government. In doing so, he allows individuals to get on with their own business governed by legal rather than moral obligation. Nevertheless, his individuals are members of a body politic, (Locke 1698 and 1956: 87) as C B Macpherson (1962) puts it, 'their individualism is necessarily collectivism' and yet again we find a tension between opposing poles as a feature of the liberal tradition. On the one hand individuals are regarded as having freedoms of various kinds but always within a constraining framework which guarantees those freedoms.

In more recent years, Locke has been reformulated in the deontological liberalism of Rawls (1972) and Nozick (1982) each of whom begins with the idea of 'radically situated' individuals in the sense that as Cartesian selves, they are rooted only in their own self-consciousness. Their initial existence owes nothing to society.

Rawls' purpose is to design a universally valid rational society, that is to say, a model which *any* rational person would design. Such a society by definition would be free from ideology and it would be self-evidently acceptable by consent. Such acceptance would represent a perfect example of free choice, unfettered by any contingencies.

In order to achieve this state of affairs, Rawls relies upon a theoretical abstraction called, 'the veil of ignorance', behind which his individuals can deliberate free from any awareness of their own interests or other contingencies which might distort their thinking. What they produce in these circumstances would be legitimated in two ways:

1)   the result would be an act of free choice;
2)   such a choice would be rational.

What emerges, and of course it is Rawls (1972: 124) who produces it: and *he* is *not* behind a veil of ignorance, is a society based on 'justice', but it is a 'distributive' concept of justice based upon the principle of greatest equal liberty and the principle of equal opportunity. It is a concept of justice uniquely adapted to be a regulatory principle for the distribution of welfare and economic goods.

Unlike the Athenians who construed their goals politically, Rawlsian individuals construe their goals and goods economically in a market. The rationality involved is a market rationality which in principle balances marginal utilities between competing individuals. A further refinement is the incorporation of a 'rights ethic' supported by a legal framework of rights defining, and rights protecting, procedures. There are no overriding public 'goods' beyond such procedures and the prime shared value is the right to choose.

An individual's right to the possession of goods (property in Locke's terminology) is justified by Nozick (1974: 151) in an 'entitlement theory' which states that a given distribution is 'just . . . if everyone is entitled to the holdings they possess' and the entitlement is defined in terms of the manner in which possessions are acquired, and this means that the appropriate legal regulatory procedures should have been followed.

This is all very clearly a set of views which are highly consistent with free market economics and every principle expressed by Rawls and Nozick is presupposed or implied within various branches of the liberal tradition. The authors are not neutral, they are already liberals, committed to a number of values before they start. Their alleged rational choices made behind the veil of ignorance are not neutrally made. They are the choices of already committed liberals in a particular historical context and the problems which they are addressing are problems which liberals would recognise as problems.

What is important from our present point of view, is the direction in which the liberal tradition has moved. It is no longer 'beneficent' in Mill's sense, nor corporate in the Athenian sense of contributing to a good society. It envisages instead a society which has tried to reduce its shared values to legal frameworks and regulatory procedures.

What is significant in this kind of theorising is the shift in emphasis away from individuals as members of society to which they make a positive contribution. This shift involves a demoting of the idea of public good in favour of private goods as the overriding priority. The private domain is given higher moral status simply because, within it, 'goods' are defined and chosen by individuals. But what appears as a moral claim is also a political claim to support the idea of minimal government. This is not an end in itself, however, it is a move towards the development of individualism.

Attempts have been made to root the new moral position entirely within a single principle, and an example is Ayn Rand, an American writer whose ideas are scattered in her novels and essays. Her general position is discussed in two articles, one by Nozick (1982: 231) and one by Douglas Den Vyl and Douglas Rasmussen (1982:232-269). The arguments are complex but they seem to be reducible to the following propositions which attempt to make 'life' the ultimate and irreducible value:

1)   life is an ultimate end, an end in itself for any living thing;
2)   to be a living thing, and not to be a living thing of a particular kind, is impossible;
3)   the particular kind of living thing an entity is determines what one must mean when talking of life with respect to a given entity;
4)   thus life as the kind of thing it is, is the ultimate value for each living thing (Den Vyl and Rasmussen 1982: 257).

Points 1) and 4) are value judgements while 2) and 3) are truisms. To have an 'end' presupposes that only sentient living things are included in 1), while 4) implies that the kind of life referred to is both sentient and rational and can, therefore, rank order its values, or as Nozick (1974: 207) puts it, can have 'a rational preference pattern'. Therefore, we are talking about human beings as persons and Nozick concludes that *'life as a rational* person is a value to the person whose life it is'.

Den Vyl and Rasmussen (1982: 250) conclude that being rational entails the ability to formulate and use concepts, by which they mean 'acting in accordance with conceptual judgements' to sustain one's own existence. 'Thus a precondition for living the life of a rational animal is that within *any* given context one must be *free from interference* upon acting according to one's judgement' (my italics).

A further point is made by Rand herself who, in arguing that the achievement of a happy existence is a person's highest aim, writes that:

'Happiness is that state of consciousness which proceeds from the achieve-ment of one's values. If a man values productive work, his happiness is the means of his success in the service of his life. But if a man values . . . mindless kicks . . . *his* alleged happiness is the measure of his success in the service of his own destruction . . . and when one experiences the kind of pure happiness that is an end in itself — the kind that makes one think: "This is worth living for" — what one is greeting and affirming in emotional terms is the metaphysical fact that *life* is an end in itself.' (Quoted Den Vyl and Rasmussen, 1982: 262.)

A number of comments might be made about this kind of argument:

1)   it makes personal judgement and freedom to act upon it an implied right because our humanity depends upon it;

2)   despite the affirmation of 'rationality', the ultimate achievement for a human being (despite our freedom to destroy ourselves if we choose), is ultimately a psychological sense of happiness or 'joy';

3)   nevertheless, striving to achieve this sense of joy is the only rational thing for a human being to do. The final goal itself is non-rational as it must be if it has no purpose beyond itself.

The significance of all this for our present purposes is to illustrate but one attempt to move the liberal tradition in the direction of individualism. The goal is no longer the good society, or democratic government or any other political goal. The final achievement is located in individuals themselves. It need not follow that they are excluded from acting, say, as 'citizens' if that makes them happy, but they need not do so. Moreover, the only moral constraint to be imposed is that of Mill's, which requires such individual to have freedom to act on his or her own judgement. By implication, this means freedom in all respects except those cases in which an action impedes that of another person. We have not quite arrived at anarchy but we appear to be very close to it. We should also note the similarity between the Randian and the Rawlsian argument in that each stresses the importance of personal preferences and that both are products of the early 1970s.

In terms of changing rationalities within the liberal tradition, we may describe the new rationality in terms of seeking personal satisfaction. There can still be a place for corporate action and individual acts of self-sacrifice, but the justification for them is in the 'joy' which they give to the actor.

Alasdair MacIntyre (1988: 338) expresses the new mood in the following terms:

' . . . in the liberal public realm individuals understand each other and themselves as each possessing his or her own ordered schedule of preferences . . . Each individual therefore, in contemplating prospective action, has first to ask . . . "What are my wants?" The answers . . . provide the initial premise for the practical reasoning of such individuals expressed as an utterance of the form, "I want it to be the case that such and such" or of some closely cognate form.'

Preference individualism, as we might now call it, has replaced 'I ought ... ' with 'I want' and this is a very different ethical claim.

The new claim in its barest form carries no implication of relationships, of citizenship or membership of society. Such things are now mechanisms which might be useful but they are not of inherent value.

However, although the emphasis might now be more extreme, there are still echoes of John Locke, and it is this kind of connection which enables us to place our various examples within the same tradition.

One of the issues now raised is how each individual arrives at a sense of his or her identity. The new injunction is akin to that of Ibsen's character whose cry is 'to thine own self be true', which in modern terms is expressed by the concept of 'authenticity'. But how do we arrive at it? What does it consist of?

The problem of authenticity

In Rawlsian terms, we have been left with a very thin definition of the self which consists of little more than the 'I' which thinks or the Kantian centre of consciousness and 'will'. If our individual is unfettered by contingency where does one begin when defining authenticity?

Charles Taylor (1992: 33) has suggested that a menu of languages is a prerequisite and these are 'not only the words we speak but also other modes of expression in terms of which we define ourselves'. This suggestion immediately brings in a social frame of reference because, by definition, a language is a medium of communication. Individuals may attempt to modify existing languages but if they are too novel communication breaks down.

The danger of this happening has been discussed by Lyotard (1979) as one of our modern (or postmodern?) dilemmas. The search for novelty, in his view, has produced a plurality of modes of expression which are the languages of particular groups. This he suggests leads to the destruction of generally available languages which are an important social bond. The idea of a 'culture' is expressible in terms of such bonds, but we are, he claims, moving towards a culture of subcultures. Individuals and members of subgroups are encouraged to be self-defining but 'each of us knows that our self does not amount to much'. Despite a narrow view of 'self', authenticity becomes more easily recognisable because we are now more mobile within a 'fabric of relationships ... [and] ... a person is always located at nodal points'. We are, he claims, all capable of taking part in *some* language games within which novel moves can be made but we only come to temporary resting places and human freedom becomes the freedom to be permanently making other moves. As a result, temporary contractual relationships become a cultural norm and we never arrive at absolute or permanent authenticity. We might each be a player in a language game but most are in very minor leagues, while the major discourses are beyond reach under the control 'of experts of all stripes' (Lyotard 1979: 15).

Taylor (1992: 35) reinforces this pessimistic view by pointing out that in order to define ourselves we need 'as background, some sense of what is significant in my difference from others', but when all social indicators are fluid we become less sure of ourselves. 'Horizons of significance' are blurred and we fly blind. 'Significant for me' becomes the only criterion and individuality becomes expressible in trivial and bizarre ways — each deemed equally worthy because they are self-selected. But the result is an individualism which is politically worthless.

Some political implications

Both Dworkin and Taylor draw attention to changes in democratic politics and they reflect two things. One is a growing preoccupation with the procedural functions of government as part of a process of 'rolling back the State'. At most, the function of government is to provide regulating frameworks rather than a vision of the future and it is particularly manifest in Britain today that Parliament is an institution for pushing through legislation without much debate. The second change is an increasing reliance on judicial review as a means of testing executive decisions. The courts rather than opposition parties are the mechanisms for challenging legislation.

In the USA judicial review is written into the Constitution, therefore at one level the courts are taking the constitution as a datum. The question is simply whether a piece of legislation is consistent with the constitution. The position in practice is not so clear-cut because there are what Dworkin (1986: 35) refers to as 'interpretive and non-interpretive theories of judicial review', and the liberal tradition must favour the former because it is more open-ended. As Dworkin rightly says, 'no-one proposes judicial review as if on a clean slate'. Law itself has a history and a tradition and successive reviews build on previous interpretations in the light of current circumstances. Constitutions, like the Bible, have a fixed text but a changing significance or meaning. Interpretation by the courts is therefore a dual process of interpreting the constitution and also the new legislation in the light of the first interpretation. However, the courts may not influence or make substantive political decisions which are the prerogative of democratically elected politicians. This is a delicate line to tread and Dworkin (1986: 58) quotes the following principles to be observed:

1)   judicial review should be a matter of attending to the *process* of legisla-
         tion rather than the outcomes considered in isolation from that process
         (my italics);

2)   it should test that process against the standard of democracy.

This is pure deontological liberalism. It is concerned with the regulation of governmental powers and it emphasises process. In such a system, it is the manner in which executive decisions are arrived at which legitimates them rather than any moral content which might be involved and it is the *procedures* which are normative for the system. The basis of this system might be called a 'procedural concept of justice', or as Agnes Heller (1987: 231) describes it, 'dynamic justice' which adapts to changing circumstances. No-one can forecast what form future judicial decisions will take beyond expecting them to conform to the tradition within which the system was developed and it is another example of liberalism in tension. The judicial review system is open-sided and creative yet constrained procedurally.

There is still a further question, however, about the nature of democracy which is one of Dworkin's procedural standards. The question is raised by John Ely who is quoted by Dworkin. He questions the normative principle itself by questioning whether there is one correct conception of 'democracy' on which to judge both judicial and political decisions and the answer is that there cannot be. There appear to be two reasons for this — one empirical and the other theoretical.

Empirically there is no agreed consensus on the precise nature of 'democracy', nor could there be without erecting the concept on absolute value or 'good' and this is theoretically unacceptable. Successive generations must be allowed to make their own interpretation. But the consequence of this must be that the courts, in making decisions on what counts as democracy do what they should not do. The courts engage in substantive politics by defining for the present, what democracy is.

These points reinforce the general contention that deontological liberalism hovers between not wishing to admit the possibility of absolute values while retaining such values in order to provide a substantive frame of reference. This difficulty can, it seems, be resolved only by recognising that we are brought back to political decisions at every turn. This is why the liberal tradition throughout the twists and turns of its history has one central theme which helps to define the tradition. That theme is the containment and control of power with a strong preference for doing so by diffusing or distributing power.

If we ask why there is this preference, we introduce yet more foundational values, such concepts as liberty, freedom, equality, rights, justice and law. If we then ask, 'Why these particular values?' the answer surely must be that behind these there is a commitment to preserving something called 'individuality' and I suggest that this commitment is the basic criterion for placing particular theories and practices within the liberal tradition.

As I have tried to show in this briefest of sketches, there are various ways of looking at the nature of 'individuality' which, like 'democracy', is open to interpretation and alternative definition. It can also be given different weightings in relation to the equally ambiguous concept of 'society'.

'The tradition' that has been the subject of this essay can never, on its own terms, provide absolute answers to any of our questions or to its own, and that is why it is a tradition and not a finite system. It cannot be the latter without producing a totally coherent philosophical case which immediately destroys its own premise that there should not be such a case because it would be inconsistent with individuality and liberty.

But as we have observed, there is one fundamental principle to be preserved and that is the moral commitment to 'individuality', and this is a practical as well as a theoretical issue. This gives us reason to conclude that moral ideas and politics intertwine with each other and with philosophy which clarifies and defines, but of itself cannot provide foundations, partly because it is unable to do so but also because the liberal tradition cannot allow it to do so.

The change of emphasis from individuality to individualism reduces the possibility of shared values or at least it reduces their number. In doing so, this makes the question of values much more a matter of private concern. 'Individualism' defined as a move to absolute autonomy or authenticity reduces the area of the self by squeezing out the social dimension and reducing the 'horizon of significance'. In diminishing the self, as Agnes Heller (1987: 304) expresses it, 'the more we liberate ourselves from all norms, the more we proceed with the unmaking of the self, the more we become unfree [and] .. the person left without norms, without authorities' ceases to have any grounds on which to reason. Like MacIntyre's person, he or she is reduced to 'I want' and is driven like the child by external stimuli and at random.

We might ask whether the liberal tradition has reached its outer limits with individualism and a radically instead of a socially located self. I suggest that it has and is in danger of destroying itself. For today's individualist this might not matter except for the fact that only within society and its norms can there be any notion of rights or of institutions to uphold them. Minimal government on deontological lines can do that job but a minimal society with minimal values is a different matter. It cannot under any circumstances have a meaningful vision.

Liberalism in adult education
There is a very extensive literature on the concept of liberal adult education and in this concluding section it is intended to do no more than illustrate points of

contact with the political liberal tradition.

Within the tradition of analytical philosophy of education (A P E), the impression is often given that liberal education is the only form of true education. R W K Paterson (1979: 38) was thus able to say that 'liberal adult education is not a species of education, it *is* education'. (My italics). But such claims can only be made within the liberal tradition which requires a form of education consonant with the idea of a liberal person as 'autonomous' or 'free' in some sense of that word. Claims of universality for liberal education can only be made if it is assumed that liberal values are themselves universal. Empirically, this clearly is not the case, neither is there a single definition of 'liberalism' and that is our reason for referring to a 'tradition'.

The Great Tradition, as debated and expounded by H C Wiltshire (1956 and 1976: 31), was context-bound, especially in the way in which 'education for citizenship' and the idea of 'individuals as social beings' were given prominence. When we put together with A P E concepts of liberal education such as the development of persons, the development of autonomy and of understanding, based on the forms of knowledge, we have what I call a 'classical concept' of liberal adult education because of its affinities with the ideals of Classical Greece. Many of these ideals entered the adult education canon via such writers as Cardinal Newman, whose ideas have elsewhere been shown to have affinities with the writings of H C Wiltshire (see A H Thornton, 1976).

The central point about the classical tradition for our present purpose is the idea of autonomy and freedom as being generated within, and as a result of, committed membership of a society with shared values. It is these which are a normative precondition for the liberal ideas of freedom and autonomy. Individuality is explicable only in terms of community.

Connections between classical liberal adult education and Mill are also apparent. Mill's individuals were held to have responsibility for the interests of others and the furtherance of such interests provided the only valid reason for interfering with the sovereignty of individuals.

In these various ways classical liberal education was a counterpoint to political and social concepts.

A marked contrast may be seen in 'modern' or deontological liberalism which stresses 'rights' rather than social responsibility and explicitly rejects the idea of a 'public good'. This is liberalism which is in harmony with views of adult education which have been described as 'libertarian', and having an affinity with existentialism. To some extent, although based on other grounds, Knowles' theories of andragogy point in the same direction by concentrating upon 'self-direction'.

Deontological principles are implicit in adult education slogans such as 'student choice', 'personal growth' and 'process before content', all of which represent attempts to be value-free. The choices about learning are legitimised by personal preferences rather than by conformity with normative values. The logic is MacIntyre's 'I want' rather than 'I ought' although this argument does not itself preclude the possibility that choices can and might be made from an existing menu of socially-expressed values. The only requirement is that they need not be.

In practice, a menu of educational 'offerings' is common in adult education and choice is confined to 'which one' of the options on offer. It is the logic of the market place and education is a commodity to be purchased, rather than a public good.

This is all consistent with the deontological form of liberalism which implicitly postulates a plurality of values, none of which are binding, beyond the value of 'self' and the rights maintaining procedures, which enshrine a procedural concept of justice.

There is a remarkable congruity between theory and practice, indicating and illustrating the manner in which each informs and reinforces the other in a dynamic way, and has the idea of 'change' incorporated within it. To that extent, the deontological view is well within the liberal tradition which has become very open-ended and liberating in one respect, but there is a false freedom to the extent that choice, from an individual point of view is criterionless, except in the limited sense that a given choice creates, or is seen to have the potential for creating, personal satisfaction.

We might ask whether this position represents a terminus for the liberal tradition, which having eschewed even the desirability as well as the possibility of a public good, can have no vision of its future. Logically, it appears to have two main options. The first is to move towards a plurality of values which is totally disintegrating. The second, which may well follow the first, is to retreat to a more normative position which constrains the expression of individuality and might well become authoritarian.

The liberal tradition is locked into its tensions because they are inherent in its original presuppositions, namely, that there must be government, but government must be contained within limits. Liberal adult education faces a similar dilemma. It seeks to be open and value-free, but values are necessary in order that choices might be meaningful and deemed rational. Some degree of social cohesion and purpose is a necessary condition for its existence and the resolution of this tension is a very political issue.

5

The concept of 'moral obligation' as an ethical foundation of liberal adult education

Introduction

In preceding essays I explored the hypothesis that theories of 'deontological' or 'rights based' liberalism provide a foundation for liberal adult education. The link between the political and educational theories of liberalism is important for the concept of 'individuality' as a foundational value. By 'individuality' I do not mean 'individualism' because with liberalism the idea of a 'social contract' binds individuals together in a common endeavour. It requires of necessity a sense of 'mutuality' based upon voluntary agreement and supported by appropriate institutions of which 'morality' is one example.

When facing moral questions about 'what ought to be done?' or in educational terms 'what should be learned?', it is assumed that answers can be provided without recourse to any idea of 'the good' as something defined independently and objectively binding. Values are deemed to be arrived at by common agreement on the belief that 'no man can judge what is good for another'. All must participate in agreeing on what is good for *them*.

Social contracts thus conceived, have a protective device built into them in the form of 'rights and duties' as legal and political concepts. They also imply that ethical values as embedded in moral codes which regulate behaviour, are enforceable by an internal sense of 'obligation'. To recognise 'an obligation' is to be aware of a constraint, but one that is voluntarily accepted rather than something like Kant's 'categorical imperative' which in some sense is external and objective.

Within a system based upon what I shall refer to as 'the deontological principle', moral and political constraints are accepted as the price of 'freedom' in other directions. One such constraint is the idea of 'citizenship' which itself entails obligations to take on the role of 'citizen' in return for the protective status of 'citizenship'. A liberal society is therefore not value free, but the values on which it is based are the minimum required as a precondition for a democratic society. They form the ground-rules or procedural frameworks within which disagreements are resolved, and competing or conflicting choices made by individuals are reconciled as a system of trade-offs designed to give all parties the best possible outcome in the circumstances. In theory, there should be no zero-sum outcomes.

The system is based upon the existence of tensions of which the most fundamental is between the perception of a radically situated self, concerned with self-interest and a philosophy of individualism on the one hand, and a socially located, cooperative and benevolent self on the other. The mediating values are those such as 'justice', 'fairness', 'equality', 'trust' and 'commitment' behind which is a 'morality of obligation'. Our immediate concern is about the adequacy of the latter, its connections with the idea of 'citizenship' and finally with the implications for liberal adult education which has within it tensions arising from its concern for the development of individuality and with citizenship.

The Morality of Obligation

This is a familiar theme in recent discussion about ethics, and both Williams (1993 and 1995) and Taylor (1995) define the 'morality of obligation' as a subsection of ethics which in practice, has come to be regarded as the whole. Taylor sees 'morality' as a guide to *action* and as such it is concerned with what it is right to do rather than what it is *good to be*. This is an important distinction which breaks with a tradition reaching back to Aristotle which links ethics to the search for values. In contrast, a morality based upon the single principle of 'obligation' is reduced to the status of a pragmatic and utilitarian regulator. It takes people as they are and seeks only to control them without making any attempt to improve them, or to be more precise, the only 'improvement' deemed to be necessary is the development of a respect for 'obligation' as a fundamental moral principle. The 'morality of obligation' is therefore based upon the most minimal or 'thin' conception of 'the good' deemed necessary for the ordering of social relationships. Behind this thinking, there is yet another value, and that is the value of 'individuality' itself. MacIntyre (1993) is correct in saying that in such views there are no moral practices beyond 'obligation' which have values internal to themselves and to that extent the 'morality of obligation' is congruent with the 'deontological principle' which goes beyond the narrowly moral, into the politico-legal domain by introducing 'right' and 'duties'. These act as supports for the concept of 'obligation', and the distinction between them is so finely drawn that it is not clear which has logical priority. For Kantians, 'duty' is fundamental, but as a prerequisite for rather than as a part of 'morality'. The concept of 'duty' evades the tautologous question 'why should we be obliged to 'obligations', because 'duty' itself commits us'. In order to avoid a question begging regression however, 'obligation' theorists in effect, resort to a consequentialist solution. The justification for making 'obligation' the primary *moral* concept rather than the primary philosophical concept is evident once we ask 'what should be the consequences of *not* having a concept of "obligation"'? As we observed this is a pragmatic solution.

The more fundamental issue is whether it is possible to have a value free society, or at least one with only the pragmatically necessary minimum required by the very idea of a regulated form of life, which is part of what is meant by a 'society'. This is the problem addressed by deontological liberalism which is an attempt to establish a society as a collection of autonomous individuals each with their own values, yet each individual having to relate to others for mutual support and protection. We are back to the Hobbesian problem and to Lockean solutions, the basis of which is 'agreements' embedded in 'contracts'.

The concept of 'obligation' arises from the idea of an agreement which has binding force. Its legal expression is the 'contract' to which the parties involved commit themselves by consent. Individuals may choose whether to agree or not on particular issues but an 'obligation' is the cement which is seen as being 'objective' to the parties concerned. It is a part of a liberal culture which for them is a 'given'. There can be no choice where an obligation is concerned once it is *accepted as* an obligation. There can be debate about the force of particular obligations, but once it is agreed that an obligation exists, it would be contradictory for parties to the agreement to refuse to honour it. To do so would be roughly equivalent to accepting the truth of a statement and then refusing to believe it. In this sense, the word 'obligation' is a linguistic indicator that commitments of some kind are recognised. The strength of the obligation derives from the agreement, which may be tacit, in standard cases such as the making of promises which are definable as the establishment of an 'obligation'. The family of terms such as 'promising', 'entering into an obligation', 'acquiring a duty' or a 'responsibility' are all a part of the discourse of 'morality' referred to as a 'morality of obligation' and each expression derives meaning from being a part of what Wittgenstein called 'language games'. To understand an expression is to understand them all, and as Williams (1985) puts it, they 'provide notable reliability, by offering a formula that will confer deliberative priority on what otherwise might not receive it'. Some things, such as a respect for life, truth telling, warning someone of an imminent danger and so on are so interwoven in a common culture that they are already established as moral obligations, and the practical problem arises over new or less clear cut cases.

Of the cases mentioned, they are given moral priority because they represent practices and dispositions which are a part of a form of life in which mutual respect and reliability are essential in order to make the social system work. None of the things that are valued require justification beyond the system because they are inherent in it. Despite claims to the contrary, there **is** a definition of the good inherent in the whole liberal system. The form of life, is itself 'the good' and it rests upon the foundation of 'individuality'. 'The morality of obligation' is of pragmatic value because it helps to maintain the system, and in that sense 'morality' is derivative. It is of value because of its function.

At one level, the 'morality of obligation' is maintained by a recognition of self-interest and the necessity of mutual reciprocation in relationships. On the system's own terms, an obligation can override any other values, and to use Taylor's (1995) expression, 'the only thing that can trump an obligation is another obligation' as when my promise to meet a friend, is overridden by a duty to attend to an emergency which puts someone in danger. This is where a disposition to act 'responsibly' in the making of judgements is a necessary precondition.

Clearly there can be no obligation to display a 'disposition'. One may be disposed to act in certain ways or not and a psychological state is not the kind of thing to which the idea of an 'obligation' applies and some dispositions at least seems not to be under our direct control. They are part of the way we are. On the other hand some dispositions might be developed and it might be regarded as one of the tasks of moral education to encourage such development. It is however, quite possible to ignore an obligation and to break an obligation for reasons which are not publicly acceptable and while we talk of persons acting 'irresponsibly' or 'failing to act responsibly' there is also a sense in which we cannot escape 'responsibility' because being responsible or more precisely 'being *held* responsible' is not a disposition. It is a judgement upon an individual, made by others. *They* say that 'I am responsible for' my actions, attitudes and so on and I am 'held to be responsible' by them. It is they who impute blame, and in some cases impose penalties. Obligations can be ignored but a price has to be paid when they are, and 'moral' obligations merge with 'legal' obligations. A more direct penalty might be the practical consequences of ignoring or breaking an obligation. A trader might lose customers, agreements might not be renewed and so on and in risking such outcomes, an individual does take responsibility upon himself. In general however, a system of 'moral obligation' is maintained by the threat of sanctions and a fear of possible consequences. Moral blame and condemnation is one of the sanctions.

It follows from this analysis that a society based upon a system of 'moral obligation' need not concern itself with developing moral propensities and dispositions. There need be no direct concern for the kinds of person its members are. They are not expected to be morally 'good' provided only that individuals follow the rules implicit in the system of 'moral obligation'. If the rules are not followed they will be blamed or they will suffer the consequences of ignoring obligations. Moral education is restricted to teaching what obligations exist and are expected and this might be called 'moral knowledge'. There is no necessity to move into the affective domain and cognitive awareness is sufficient. But on a broader view of ethics, this limitation might be regarded as a weakness. On the basis of the deontological principle however, these limitations are a strength because the 'morality of obligation' places weight entirely upon the choices actually made by individuals who pay the price for any adverse consequences. Self interest becomes the main social regulator, and the question 'what ought I to do?' does not put any moral weight on 'ought' in that term. I am expected to place the question in a framework of obligations, but whether or not the relevant obligation is recognised and accepted, is purely a personal decision dependent upon an assessment of consequences. I need not *feel* 'obliged' in particular circumstances despite the fact that others argue that I am and this demonstrates the importance of the idea of 'agreement'. What others regard as obligations have also to be accepted by me and this feature is consistent with the 'deontological principle' by leaving the final decision with individuals. In short an 'obligation' only becomes an obligation when it is mutually accepted and recognised as such. I might still have on occasion a personal *sense* of obligation in some circumstances, but this does seem to be a 'true' obligation in the sense that the system requires it.

Williams (1993) claims that a 'moral obligation is inescapable and allows no emigration' and this seems to imply that the force of an obligation is one-sided and does not depend upon mutual recognition. It appears as it were as an objective fact to be taken into account by any individual. Obligations are already laid down, but on the arguments set out above, this is only true in a general sense and what matters is whether or not particular concrete obligations here and now are accepted by me. Until they are accepted they are only putative obligations for *me* but they are inescapable in the sense that others are likely to blame me for ignoring or not accepting particular obligations. We can therefore distinguish between 'obligations in principle' such as the keeping of promises, honouring agreements and contracts, recognising treaties, helping people in distress and so forth, and 'substantive obligations' agreed in specific cases. Once accepted by all parties involved as 'obligations to them' they cannot without contradiction be ignored.

But individuals do as a matter of fact refuse to recognise obligations without contradiction because for them it simply is not regarded as an obligation and one cannot be accused of contradiction after denying that an obligation exists. Kant tried to establish that morality *per se* was an unconditional imperative which as Williams put it 'goes all the way down', but we *are* concerned here with specific putative obligations *within* a conception of morality and about which there can be disagreement. I might risk being ostracised and condemned for refusing to act in what other people regard as a 'moral' way and from a public point of view I *am* immoral although from my point of view I am guiltless because I perceive no obligation to be honoured. It would seem therefore that we imagine a system of morality based upon the concept of 'obligation' as universally agreed but which admits the possibility of disagreement on what substantive obligations should be recognised. The possibility of disagreement, represents disagreement on *values* (is 'x' worthy of becoming an obligation?) and this is consistent with the deontological principle which is based on a claim that values cannot be imposed on others. I am on this principle entitled to my own opinion. I have a right to it. Williams is correct in asserting that 'moral obligation is inescapable and allows no emigration' only in relation to the general principle of obligation. In specific cases, about which an individual disagrees on whether something counts as an obligation he or she is not bound, although what is inescapable, is the possibility of moral condemnation incurred as a consequence of having independent judgement.

Williams has noted that some moralists admit to a category of 'self-obligation' as when I say that 'I owe it to myself' to behave in a particular way but on the arguments already considered, an obligation is always an obligation to someone beyond myself. It is essentially a public concept but it breaks down and ceases to function when someone is sufficiently strong minded, to stand aloof from the general will.

Such a person is condemned as immoral because of his or her refusal to recognise obligations where others do so. For such a person no obligation exists as for example when faced by putative obligations to what is seen as an immoral state or governmental policy. In such a case, no defence is allowed except a stronger obligation and in the absence of agreement on what this might be, the only recourse available is to argue in terms of a higher good which might include the idea of an ethical value such as a 'moral conscience'. The person who does this is faced with a dilemma. Personal expression of values has been made in accordance with the deontological principle of free choice, yet in isolation our dissenting individual cannot establish (an agreed) obligation to give priority to a moral conscience, which is not accepted as an intrinsically valuable and desirable characteristic. As Taylor (1995) observes, the 'morality of obligation' allows no scope for 'what it is good to be' as distinct from 'what it is right to do' and there is no room either for acts of 'superogation' which go beyond the demands of obligation such as 'acts of courage or self-dedication'. Such acts in political contexts are not simply of no value under the principle of obligation, they might actually be criminalised and the morality of obligation can lead to an oppressive conformity which is anti-liberal, and leaves no place for virtue.

This conclusion follows from the narrow logic of a system based on mutual assent and which paradoxically, might otherwise be seen as a powerful antidote to the excessive radical individualism also inherent in deontological liberalism. There are implications in this for the concept of 'citizenship' as a limitation upon freedom and beyond that there are also implications for liberal adult education but it is to 'citizenship' that we now turn.

The Concept of Citizenship as a Constraint

The preceding discussion highlights ways in which a system of morality establishes constraints and this is precisely what a moral code is intended to do. It is a part of a regulatory system within which the concepts of 'obligation', 'duties', 'rights' and 'law' are component parts of a social system. Their existence in all societies in some form or other, demonstrates the impossibility of total pluralism in respect of values and the principles which determine choices and actions. The necessity of social regulators and mechanisms for establishing common causes is also recognised in the political concept of 'citizenship' which implies 'membership' and it has two dimensions. It represents a *status* which implies 'protection', 'privileges' and 'rights'. It also carries corresponding 'responsibilities', 'obligations' and 'duties' and the acceptance of a *role* and the political and ethical theories behind the concept of 'citizenship' draw analogies between membership of the 'state' and 'society' and membership of 'a club' as a defining metaphor.

The tension involved in the 'liberal' models of society and the state which are also posited on the concept of 'individuality' are evident in Rawl's (1972) concept of 'equal liberty' but which cannot be 'total liberty'. The tension is resolved if it is possible to establish 'equality of constraint' and this for Rawls puts the emphasis upon the idea of 'justice as fairness' as a regulatory criterion. There are three main areas in which a citizen must make judgements:

1) Legislation, political and economic policies.
2) The mechanisms and procedures for reconciling conflicts and disagreements.
3) The grounds and limits of political and ethical values and decisions.

The citizen is in effect, given the responsibility for deciding upon the scope and limits of freedom both in a broad abstract sense, and in particular concrete cases. This is a considerable demand to make and it presupposes (a) an ability to make the necessary judgements and to participate in decision making procedures, (b) access to the appropriate information and conceptual knowledge, and (c) a willingness and a commitment to participate in the various procedures, either directly or by electing representatives. An appropriate educational system is also implied, not as an optional extra, but as an essential requirement.

The Obligation of Citizenship

The nature of possible or putative obligations is set out above but a central question is about the strength of the overall obligation to accept the role of 'citizen'. In one sense, it must be an absolute obligation which 'reaches all the way down', yet on the basis of earlier arguments, to be an 'obligation' it has to be freely and mutually recognised and accepted. It is an option which is necessary yet it cannot be a forced option, because 'responsibility' freely acquired and exercised is necessary to establish an obligation, and this is a paradox of the concept of 'obligation'. It only has moral force because it is accepted as having moral force. It is an indicator which signifies that a commitment has been made whereas it appears to be the 'cause' or the reason for making a commitment. We do not say 'here is an obligation, I must honour it' but rather 'I am committed to doing such and such *therefore* it becomes an obligation'. It signifies my goodwill and sincerity. This suggests that obligations do not create moral situations, thus the making of a promise is a morally relevant act which establishes an implied contract in a culture where 'promises as contracts' are expected to be honoured and to describe a promise as carrying or entailing an obligation is to impose a contract upon an existing contract. The obligation is a linguistic device to underscore the original contract or to emphasise it.

In everyday speech, standard examples such as 'promises', 'agreements', 'respect for life', 'respect for authority' and 'acceptance of the demands of citizenship' are all members of a category of values which carry a *prima facie* status of carrying an obligation but they do so because they are already highly valued as a general rule. But, in particular cases they can be overridden by higher values deemed to carry a stronger obligation. For someone who chooses not to accept a particular putative obligation it does not count as an 'obligation'.

From a Rawlsian or deontological liberal point of view, rejection of, or a refusal to admit the existence of a particular obligation, is quite legitimate, because individuals are deemed to have the right to 'determine the grounds and limits of political duty and obligation'. This leaves the concept of 'citizenship' very exposed because it is possible to ignore its demands except in the case of such examples as the payment of taxes which are seen as legally, not morally binding. Indeed, it is a common complaint that the demands of citizenship are not taken seriously. They are not regarded as obligations, in any strong sense, although individuals may still take refuge in the idea of having 'rights' which they hope will be seen as obligating other people. Among such rights is the 'right to dissent' and from one point of view, that of the dissenter, such a right carries an obligation by others to respect dissent when it occurs, and this might be justified as a 'negative' form of citizenship which allows individuals *pace* the British 'Poll Tax revolt' to reject particular governmental decisions and policies. It is a nice question, whether such 'negative' aspects of 'citizenship' could become 'obligations' because of the difficulty of determining who are the relevant parties to such an obligation. Can two or more individuals establish what for them is an obligation to dissent, which in effect is to the detriment of a third party? The strict logic of 'obligation' does not fit such cases, and morally and politically legitimate dissent is supported by a doctrine of 'rights' to which individuals are entitled, and which democratic governments have an obligation to observe and respect.

It is possible, therefore, to relate the concept of 'obligation' to political concepts such as 'citizenship', by resorting to the device of 'presumed' and 'putative obligations'. To reduce the concept of 'citizenship' to a network of 'obligations' nevertheless seems to be an impossibility. There has to be resort to a more extensive framework of values such as 'justice', 'fairness', 'equality' and so on as well as ethical values such as 'aspirations to perfection', 'heroism, superogation and the like' to which both Taylor and Williams refer. For both writers it is a mistake to attempt to reduce the whole of ethics to a single concept such as 'moral obligation'. For Taylor (1995) especially, it is important that liberal societies should be able once again, 'to talk about goods (as) as a condition of addressing . . . serious issues', and this would appear to be a view which supporters of MacIntyre's (1981) view could accept.

From Rawl's point of view this is also a legitimate position, because he attributes to individuals the right to 'determine the limits of political duty and obligation'. The latter, he regards as the result of 'voluntary acts' based upon 'tacit understandings' with particular people, but to satisfy Taylor's requirement, the reasons for agreeing to specific obligation should be based on values external to or beyond the obligation itself. 'Obligations are placed into a wider framework of values which together help to define 'a way of living' as Taylor puts it. Moral obligations are only one component of this way of life and their *relative importance* has to be assessed in the light of competing values and aspirations.

'Importance', as Williams observes is itself an ambiguous and relative concept, and we must ask 'importance to what' and 'importance to whom' type questions. Something might be important to me, an expression of a personal evaluation, but not necessarily of wider importance. Relative importance is judged in a process of ascertaining what Williams calls 'deliberative priority' which is determined by considering the different reasons for regarding something as important. There is 'personal' and 'public' importance, together with such examples as 'moral', 'aesthetic', 'economic' and 'political' importance. We consider in effect 'the importance of competing and varying degrees of 'importance'.

The Importance of 'Importance'

The concepts of 'obligation' and 'importance' share one characteristic in common. They are 'logical stops' which are used to terminate particular discussions. Once the importance of something is agreed upon within a particular community (which may be large or small) nothing further can or need be said, at least for the *time being*. A stop is imposed upon that particular conversation, but on a wider canvas varying degrees of importance might be established. In ordering deliberative priorities, 'choices', have to be made both by individuals and by groups of individuals in concert and it is only on the broadest view possible that valid decisions can be made about the public importance of lower level private decisions. An individual, as Mill (1859) claimed can only have choice in respect of that which concerns him alone, but an individual cannot be the judge on what is of private concern alone. Liberalism does not in fact attribute absolute importance to personal choices. We are obliged to ask 'what is the (relative) importance of what I think is important?'

This issue is not merely a matter of what my community or society will permit me to do. It is also a matter of logic, and we are reminded of Wittgenstein's (1953) argument that an individual cannot validly distinguish between what he or she thinks or believes is the case and what is the case. This raises issues about the nature of 'truth conditions' but for the present, this point is merely noted. We are directly concerned however with 'the logic of choice' which in the liberal framework is regarded as the culmination of a process which is rational in the sense that 'reason' can be given in support of a choice, which is more than a response to the tricksters injunction to 'take any card'. The concept of 'choice' and the act of 'choosing' have normative implications within a liberal discourse and these conflict with the deontological principle that 'no one can choose what is good for another' when it comes down to defining criteria for the act of choosing.

There are some areas of choice which are defined as 'matters of taste' which in some circumstances may be regarded as a private matter, and pure personal preferences are accepted. But what is allowed in the expression of preferences for kinds of chocolate, is not permitted in issues which raise ethical and moral questions as in the case of cruel sports, abortion or in debates about public versus private ownership of capital. In deciding or choosing on such matters we are expected to provide 'good reasons' in justification of choices. Arguments are expected to be cogent, based upon and consistent with 'evidence', 'sound opinion' and so forth. 'Rationality' defined as 'the giving of good reasons' thus becomes a complex concept which goes beyond the observance of rules of logic, although these are also included.

The further idea of 'responsibility' is introduced into the ordering of priorities and the making of choices because not all choices can be brought forward for public judgement. When acting in a private capacity there is a tacit assumption that 'responsible' decisions and choices will be made with the 'public interest' in mind, and this assumption in turn presupposes the acceptance of a shared scale of values. This might be seen as a weakening of deontological principles by admitting a range of values. There is still an assumption however, that values of all kinds, in common with the idea of 'obligation' are voluntarily accepted. This maintains the concept of 'individuality' as a foundational value, but it also enables us to draw a clear distinction between 'individuality' and 'individualism' which can be interpreted in terms of Nozick's (1974) 'individual anarchist' model and a minimal state which does no more than provide minimal protection to individuals who are not *required* to cooperate. They may choose to do so but only if there are good reasons for cooperating. They are assumed to calculate the balance of advantage, or in economists terms the 'marginal utility' arising from one course of action compared with others. They are interested in net personal gains rather than in the 'general good'.

'Rationality' as the giving of good reasons, is again emerging as a significant idea. Individuals act in the light of what *for them* are considerations of 'importance' but although such considerations are 'good reasons' for acting in particular ways they might not appear to be good reasons from the point of view of others. Negotiation and mutual acceptance of allegedly 'good reasons' must in principle be introduced, but within a web of potentially conflicting interests there is no guarantee that negotiated outcomes will be fair and therefore acceptable as an overriding 'good reason' that is to say, that it will maximise total utility or the 'greatest general good'. But 'utility' is an abstraction used in liberal economics to denote a generalised psychological 'satisfaction', and it can only be a reason for acting and a justification for actions if their consequence is in fact, likely to lead to desired consequences. This makes them 'reasons' i.e. 'rational' criteria if and only if they have the desired consequences.

In practice, and this is why there are moral codes and ethical standards, 'reasons as justifiers' are *needed* in order to assess particular concrete decisions and actions and their concrete outcomes, rather than generalised 'satisfactions' which could themselves be derived from cruel or dishonourable actions. Moral judgements may be made at each stage, including the outcomes and a 'good reason' for 'doing x' thereby making it a rational, reasoned and reasonable thing to do, requires:

a)   that the outcome be acceptable.
b)   that the intended action is consistent with the outcome (i.e. likely to achieve it by being causally related).
c)   that the action itself is acceptable.
d)   that the reason given in support of the action is also acceptable.

The term 'acceptable' is used because the deontological principle admits of no values which in the Kantian sense transcend the individuals who are participants in the moral discourse. Nevertheless, they do use concepts such as 'causal relationships', 'consistency', 'consequence', 'reasons', 'reasonable' and so on. These are all built into a shared discourse which to the participants themselves is a 'given' inherited as one of many social practices. (For a more detailed account, se e.g. S Toulmin, 1950). The discourse is the product of earlier generations and it becomes transcendental to successive generations. For them, it makes moral and ethical thought possible and in that sense it is transcendental to them, but they can if they choose, reject the values inherent in the discourse. In so doing, they take on the responsibility of facing the consequences of others who adhere to the inherited values and who are entitled to call the nonconformists 'unethical' and 'immoral' or just plain 'unreasonable'.

Rawls' theoretical attempt to establish values transcendental in the limited sense described above, yet rooted in human beings as individuals, is the fiction of a 'veil of ignorance' behind which, any human beings, unaware of their self-interest, would choose a rational, ethical and political set of values. As beings unaware of any special distinguishing characteristics, they know, as Rawls puts it 'what it means to be free and equal rational being(s)'. They display human nature as it is. They are paradigm human beings, free from all contingencies of nature which might otherwise 'influence' their choice. But such an allegedly pure 'state of nature' already presupposes a capacity for rational thought and disinterested action. It is not natural 'man' but a model of liberal human beings with which the argument begins. They are ethically, linguistically and culturally located before the argument begins. Rawls' individuals might be deemed to be ignorant but Rawls knows perfectly well where they come from, and where he wishes them to go. The 'veil of ignorance' provides a nice illustration, it is a teaching aid but it does not represent a 'state of nature'. They represent a liberal's vision of 'the good', and the arguments used by Rawls, are similar to Descartes' individual who, starting from a neutral awareness of 'self' applies a logical method of inference to establish what can be known. But the self which thinks, already possesses a language in which thoughts can be formulated. 'I am therefore I think' could not be formulated in a pre-linguistic state and Descartes knew in advance what his epistemological logical problem was and he had the tools with which to begin the construction of a possible solution.

Some Implications for Liberal Adult Education

In arguing that a 'morality of obligation' is consistent with deontological liberalism, it seems likely that there will be implications for the practice of liberal adult education. Traditionally, the latter has associated with the twin ideas of individual development and education for citizenship between which there appears to be an inherent tension. But there need not be if what I have called 'the mutuality' between individuals and society is recognised and if 'the state' is regarded as the political manifestation of society. Individuals develop their powers of thought and communication in relationships with others as well as their ethical values and moral codes of behaviour. Liberal adult education, with its practices rooted in the values and codes, is also the mechanism which evaluates and transmits the codes and values not as an optional extra but as a logical consequence of being a part of the liberal culture. It is not necessary to claim that liberal adult educators have an obligation to fulfil these roles because to be committed to liberal adult education is itself a commitment to the transmission of liberal values as a matter of definition. This puts the liberal adult educator in the role of 'missionary' already committed to a system of values.

No doubt objections will be made to this analysis and it will be claimed that educators as such should be neutral. Up to a point this *is* a valid claim but it is neutrality *within* a system and an analogy might be drawn with science, where a scientist is neutral about the eventual outcome of a piece of research, and an experiment can weaken as well as support a hypothesis. But either way, a researcher is deeply committed to the research procedures and the logical and epistemological values built into them, and as a teacher of science he or she is also committed but in a critical reflective, rather than a dogmatic, frame of mind. Liberal teachers can be critical of what they teach *as they teach it* and this includes the teaching of ethical and political values which are both transcendent to the teaching and imminent within it. To be a supporter and a critic at the same time, is an uncomfortable position to be in and this might be the reason why some people seek security in dogma. Others sit on the fence.

6

Limits to the concept of 'autonomy' as an adult education objective

Introduction

Although the concept of personal autonomy as an adult education objective has a strong emotional appeal, this essay explores the limits of this idea.

Starting from the root sense of 'autonomy' as 'self-ruling', the political origins of the idea in ancient Greek thought and in Hegel's philosophy are noted. As a characteristic of States as well as of individuals, 'autonomy' is concerned with sovereignty and independence which are quasi-contractual and status related terms. Autonomy is mutually recognised.

When seen as the ability to think and make private judgements, 'autonomy' is associated with rationality and reason, which are rule governed concepts. Wittgenstein's argument about the impossibility of private rules and private languages is applied in order to demonstrate once again the public reference and the mutuality inherent in what appears to be an individualistic concept. There is neither pure autonomy nor absolute non-autonomy.

At various points, the nature of individual identity and the concept of 'intention' are discussed and it is concluded that 'autonomy' cannot be a direct objective in adult education. Nevertheless educators can contribute indirectly to the development of autonomy by helping adults to develop relevant skills, competencies and areas of knowledge, all of which are in the realm of public practice and public procedures.

Autonomy and Non-autonomy

It might be supposed that a concept such as 'autonomy' may be understood in contrast to its opposite 'non-autonomy'. One implies an ability to choose, to make decisions, to make judgements, to 'think for oneself' and so on. It is the exercise of 'independence'. A non-autonomous person can do none of these things. But there is a sense in which in practice, both concepts are conjoined. Thus in expressing an independent thought, autonomy is constrained by language and its rules, by the options available, by ethical considerations and so on. On the other hand we are rarely totally constrained. We can break rules, we can refuse to obey an order. What is of interest is the relationship in one situation, of an element of autonomy and also an element of non-autonomy. We are neither totally free nor totally constrained. Thus in educational terms it is possible say, to develop an independent line of thought and argument, but only within limits of acceptable logic, and available concepts. In adult educational contexts, adults are deemed to be capable of choosing what they should learn, yet their choices are limited by what they already know. 'Autonomy' is expected of adult learners but it is not an absolute state. Areas in which they are not yet autonomous are deemed to exist therefore an extension of autonomy becomes a goal but there are always limits. 'Autonomous individuals' are *also* non-autonomous in some respects. We are therefore exploring conceptual limits and ambiguities.

In the literature on adult education, considerable emphasis is placed upon the concept of 'individual autonomy' as an educational objective. Examples are in Paterson (1979) and more recently in Edwards and Usher (1995) who locate the idea in a postmodern context. In order to be an *educational* objective however, it is necessary that the capacity to be, or to become autonomous is acquired by learning. If this is not the case, it is difficult to understand why autonomy should be of special interest to adult educators in contrast say, to ethical and political theorists. It is argued that only weaker constrained concepts of autonomy are of educational interest.

It will be obvious that 'autonomy' and its opposite are related to a cluster of concepts which includes 'sovereignty', 'freedom' and the ability to choose, which in turn is related to the idea of 'responsibility'. We are dealing therefore with ideas which have both a political and an ethical dimension. 'Autonomy' is held to be a desirable characteristic of human beings as 'individuals' and 'persons'. 'Autonomy' is also associated with 'reason' and 'rationality', therefore it carries a considerable semantic load and it is a key element in the discourse of 'liberalism' which helps to explain its attraction to those engaged in adult education.

The roots of the concept of 'autonomy' may be traced back to ancient Greece (see Farrar 1988). The idea emerges again in Hegel's thought (1821), it is present under the guise of 'liberty' in J S Mill (1861 and 1962) and more recently in Rawls (1991). The political antecedents are clear. It is the political realm which is autonomy's natural home. In that context 'autonomy' functions as a device for defining relationships between political groupings or states as well as relationships between individual human beings.

On the one hand it 'distances' but as a regulating ideal it also protects and ensures good relationships. What might appear to be a highly individualistic concept, at home in liberalism with radically situated 'selves', is also a communitarian concept, which has significance and meaning only where there is a plurality of individuals. For a Robinson Crusoe, the term 'autonomy' could have no meaning. We return to these points later.

Some definitions within educational contexts

Typical examples may be found in Paterson (1979) where the distinction is made between 'mental' and 'moral' autonomy, although the former is presupposed in the latter. Thus, a 'mentally autonomous person' is 'a person who thinks for himself' (p.119) but Paterson immediately recognises that this means only 'he is thinking'. The argument has not taken us very far and it still has to be explained why being able 'to think' is a sign or indication of 'mental autonomy' except in the tautologous or analytic sense that 'anyone who thinks, thinks autonomously' because it is a 'thinker who thinks'. If this is the case, then 'teaching people how to think' becomes an educational objective rather than autonomy itself.

To be regarded as 'mentally autonomous', something else must be implied by that phrase and it might help our understanding to recognise the root sense of 'autonomy' as one who is Autonomous or 'self governing' in a political and legal sense. 'Mental autonomy' then appears to be a dead metaphor which has acquired a literal meaning but it is by no means clear what is involved in being both the governed and the governor except by postulating an entity such as an 'ego' distinguishable from a 'person' yet part of our personhood.

A less misleading linguistic form is used by Paterson when he defines 'a mentally autonomous person' as 'a man of independent mind ... who forms his own judgements'. This is independence from others whose judgements are not accepted without question. Paterson (p.124) considers 'moral autonomy' is a special case of 'mental autonomy' and the source of 'responsibility'. To act on one's judgement is to act responsibly and to be held responsible for the consequences of one's action. On the other hand, it is the judgement of others which determines whether we did in fact act responsibly on a particular occasion, in the sense of giving thought to what we did. The ascription of responsibility in this evaluative sense, as well as its ascription in a moral and in legal senses, is a public, not a private matter and a communal dimension is introduced.

This dual internal-external response will be returned to later, but for the moment we note that normative expectations and requirements are attached to the idea of autonomy. It is something that individuals are expected to experience and to experience it in particular ways by 'giving thought', and having a regard for the consequences and implications of our thought and behaviour. Thus R S Peters (1973) says that 'our *normal* expectation of a person is that he is a chooser'. Elsewhere in the same collection of essays Feinberg equates being 'free' with being 'independent, self governing, autonomous' which he later expands into the idea of a 'parapolitical metaphor' which stresses the permissive as well as the normative expectations associated with the idea of being free to, and capable of, making choices.

The political dimension

Cynthia Farrar (1988) shows how the political roots of the above ideas may be located in several strands in Athenian thought. One relates to the attempt to attribute responsibility by detaching individuals from governance by 'fate', while another is concerned with liberation from the constraints of 'tradition and the demands of social order' (chapter 2 passim).

Another strand is the overtly political attempt of Athenians to free themselves from autarchy within, and from dominance by Sparta without. 'Democracy' was a device for securing internal freedom for individual citizens while 'sovereignty' was the desired attribute of states. The two strands were given a sense of unity and conceptual coherence by defining Athenians as 'citizens' as their major attribute. 'Autonomy' was already a two tier concept with both personal and societal dimensions.

A political concept of 'autonomy' also appears in Hegel's *Philosophy of Right* (English translation 1952) where in para.331 it is claimed that 'The nation state . . . is the absolute power on earth. It follows therefore, that every state is sovereign and autonomous against its neighbours and without qualification'. But this absolute view is severely qualified a few sentences later by the observation that 'autonomy is conditional upon the neighbouring states judgement and will'. Then in para.352 we find that 'the immediate actuality which any state possesses from the point of view of other states, is particularised into a multiplicity of relations which are determined by the arbitrary will of both autonomous parties, and which therefore possess the formal nature of contracts pure and simple'. This leaves us with a much weaker contractual and conditional concept of autonomy. A similar idea is also implicit in earlier passages where Hegel discusses individual or 'personal identity' and freedom, and the relationship between body and mind.

In paragraphs 48-72 it is stated that 'insofar as the body is an immediate existent, it is not in conformity with the mind. If it is to be the willing organ and soul-endowed instrument of mind, it must first be taken into possession by mind. But from the point of view of others, I am in essence a free entity in my body (which) while I am in possession of it is immediate . . . and my body is the embodiment of my freedom'.

This return to a mind body dualism from an internal point of view takes account of our ability to separate conceptually our consciousness of 'self' from our corporeal self but without having to explain the distinction. On the other hand, our freedom is embodied (literally) from the point of view of other people, who, if they choose, 'may do violence to my body'. Defence against this possible violence to the self and its 'property' lies in the existence of 'rights' established and maintained contractually. Thus 'my' will is made operable by the will of others, or more simply my wish to be free to act is conditioned by the extent to which others agree to my acting in particular ways. Once more, concepts of 'will', 'freedom' and 'autonomy' have both a subjective and an objective reference. Individuals are portrayed as not having absolute control of themselves. They are controlled by external regulations, prohibitions and licences. This is expressed in paragraph 72 which states: 'Contract is the process in which there is revealed and mediated the contradiction that I am and remain the independent owner of something from which I exclude the will of another only insofar as my identifying my will with the will of another I cease to be an owner'. This may be called 'contractual' freedom and autonomy.

In J S Mill's *On Liberty* the 'autonomy problem' is expressed in terms of 'individuality' and 'sovereignty' where the justification of 'freedom' rather than the explanation is the issue. Thus on page 109 (1962 edition) the expression 'duty to oneself . . . means self respect'. 'Liberty' is therefore justified as a precondition for the respect of both ourselves and others and this is a moral principle. For this reason 'independence' (or 'autonomy') is of right, absolute. Over himself, over his own body and mind, the individual is (or rather 'ought to be') sovereign (page 135).

Despite this stress upon sovereignty. Mill places restrictions upon the extent of permissible liberty. Sovereignty in his view should be constrained by external regulation and the problem is in defining morally and politically acceptable limits. The question concerns the rightful limit to the sovereignty of the individual over himself, and 'Where does the authority of society begin?' (p.205).

Mill's famous answer is that 'To individuality should belong the part of life in which it is chiefly the individual that is interested; to society, the part which chiefly interests society'. This is a notoriously difficult distinction to draw and for Mill the distinction in practice must be determined by 'free and equal discussion' (p.136). To be meaningful, discussion must be ordered and sequential, that is to say, it must not consist of haphazard verbalisation but of rational and intentional discourse. It must also be on terms of equality, so two new constraints have been introduced, namely 'reason' and 'equality'. By implication also, the ability to engage in reasoned discussion presupposes that the skills involved are learnable, and we move closer to the idea that such learning becomes an educational objective. As Mill (p.185) puts it:

'If it were felt that the free development of individuality is one of the essentials of well being; that it is not only a coordinate element with all that is designated by the terms civilisation, instruction, education, culture, but is itself a necessary part and condition of all those things, there would be no danger that liberty should be undervalued, and the adjustment of boundaries between it and social control would present no extraordinary difficulties'.

Liberal ideology and liberal education are so interwoven that the imposition of learning is not a constraint upon, but a means of achieving, freedom.

There is a paradox nevertheless in the idea that 'autonomy' and 'freedom' are being defined in normative terms. We are not being given the right to behave irrationally and according to our feelings or desires. We are constrained to act within a framework of rules and conventions which are publicly accepted, within a tradition. Rational autonomy therefore liberates us from our own ignorance and desires. It is yet another version of constrained, defined freedom and autonomy. As with ancient Athenian concepts, the trick as it were, is to constitute forms of freedom which, although recognising individuality, are also conducive to the maintenance of public order and the wellbeing of the state. Ostensibly sovereign individuals constitute a sovereign state by their free, voluntary actions and in this lies much of the appeal of the liberal ideology. It produces power by consent which maintains control. It is a theoretically neat solution to the problem of government by producing 'self-government' at two levels; the level of individuality and the societal level.

Individuality

The point has been made that autonomy has both an individual response and a communal response. It is a term which has meaning within a set of social relationships and from which individuals wish to distance themselves, or to establish 'private space'. But within liberal theory, priority is given to 'individuality' and this is why 'autonomy' becomes such an important concept. 'Autonomy', 'individuality' and 'personal identify' are all interrelated, and from them a sense of 'personhood' is developed.

On the Cartesian view, as in liberal theory, a pre-existent, self-conscious, self-referring 'I' is postulated as a starting point from which knowledge is constructed. This 'centre' of consciousness is in some sense 'rational' and a constant which defines self-identity. But, as Ayer (1956) argued, such a self is reduced to an empty self-referring or inward pointing, which amounts to no more than a tautological 'I am I'.

Against the apparently flawed Cartesian premise, we argue that we are born into relationships as members of families within which we are biologically individualised, and in that sense we are 'natural' but our identity is *designated* for us by our birth order, sex, name and so on. 'I' have to learn who I am *within* a family and *beyond* that in wider social categories. Thus the question 'Who am I?' and 'Who are you?' are typically given in terms of name, sex, status, occupation etc. Personal identity develops as new roles are acquired and as the range of experience is enlarged, thus a complete description of a person's identity would be a total biographical description of 'the person who . . . ' At any point, depending upon context, the questions 'Who am I?' or 'Who are you?' could be answered specifically in terms such as, 'John Doe', 'the man next door', 'leader of the County Council', 'manager of the Co-op' or whatever. We have a plurality of identities in the sense of personal and social references. The centre of consciousness is a constant but its identity is not, and this is why an identifying number as in prisons or in military contexts is regarded as so totally dehumanizing. Most of us prefer a well constructed identity and it is surely a part of the feminist case that women do not want, nor should they have a single-criterion identity as 'the wife of . . .'

Nevertheless, an individually constructed self-identity may be given in psychological terms by using the concept of 'memory'. Other people can give an account of my personal biography, but so the argument goes, only 'I' know whether it is accurate. *You* might say that 'I did x' but only *I* know whether 'I did x'. Such an argument is in effect a revival of the arguments of Descartes and Locke for a personally verifiable sense of indubitability. 'I' am the source of my own verification. My memory is deemed to be uniquely accessible.

Hamilton (1995) expresses this thesis in terms of 'memory judgements' being 'immune to error through mis-identification'. But although it is true that my memory is uniquely self-accessible it is conceptualised in order to be recalled, but 'experiences are an interpretation' and 'memory' also consists of interpretation. We do sometimes make mistakes which can be revealed by external evidence. We can and do have fake memories which convert 'I remember' into 'I apparently remember'.

There is also a sense in which we cannot remember, and this applies to what cannot be conceptualised and described. It is difficult at least, to remember a pain, and we can only *say* what a pain was *like*. We have very inadequate vocabularies with which to express feelings publicly and we cannot express them privately either.

We may conclude therefore that 'Beings' might be natural, but 'persons' are socially created by acquiring the status, dignity and rights of 'personhood'. This concept is therefore in the same category as 'adulthood' defined as a 'status' concept signifying society's expectations of adult behaviour and its corresponding rewards in terms of 'rights'. 'Who' I am as a centre of consciousness becomes merged with 'what' I am and the list of possible identifying characteristics becomes indefinitely large, because what we are depends upon the complex of roles and relationships in families, organisations and society at large. These roles and relationships may be seen from a personal point of view and from viewpoints of those with whom we have relationships. We are exemplifying our 'persona' in the Greek sense and we all play many parts, not all of which are of our own making. In a sense, the public makes us 'what we are' and we perceive ourselves in terms of what Taylor (1991) calls 'horizons of significance' which help to define self-perceptions.

Cultural norms

The idea of self-perceptions would seem to be a paradigmatic example of an area for autonomy, but Taylor's point is to suggest that we draw upon cultural norms in deciding 'what is significant in my difference from others'. To be taught what is good for us is a clear infringement of autonomy, yet even for post-modernists, choices and self-perceptions are not *ex nihilo*, they are created in cultural contexts and there are matrices from which there is no escape. As Taylor expresses it, things cannot have significance simply because individuals deem them to have it. Significance is acquired within a context and against a background (to change the simile) and the rest of the world is entitled to play a part in determining significance. To say this questions the whole concept of 'autonomy' but it supports the present thesis that at most 'autonomy' is a conditional, constrained concept.

Nevertheless, there is a sense in which our thoughts are 'ours' and it is 'I' who thinks. Both 'reason' and 'rationality' are internalised concepts as when we use the metaphors 'the inner light of reason'. In this sense 'reason' and 'rationality' are capacities that we possess and we may demonstrate them publicly. They are modes of thinking but both 'reason' and 'rationality' are evaluative terms and are applied to particular performances in a judgemental way thus as well as being 'capacities' they are also criteria. They are normative standards to which reasoned, rational thought conforms, and these standards are embedded in public traditions which embody rules of logic and grammar which is itself a kind of 'logic'.

To be accepted as 'reasoning', 'rational' beings, two conditions must be satisfied:
1)   that we know how to think rationally and to reason,
2)   that we are disposed to think and act in ways deemed to be rational and reasonable.

External reference points are introduced, and although our disposition to act in particular ways is deemed to be within our private control, and in that sense we are autonomous, we have no control over public expectations of us. On the other hand, it might be claimed that we can choose whether or not we are willing to satisfy public expectations. We are free to be irrational, eccentric and unreasonable. 'But is it possible to have private thoughts?'

In the usual sense of 'thinking' as opposed to 'intuition' we seem to have in mind a kind of 'private talking to oneself' which makes use of all the categories, terminology and grammar of public speech. Use is made of logical constants such as 'if', 'then', 'and', 'but', together with quantifiers such as 'some', 'all' and 'many'. We are still operating within learned but publicly defined parameters. We can be imaginative, creative and even 'unrealistic' in our thinking but it remains constrained in form although autonomous in content.

When our thoughts are made public in acts of communication the constraints are more rigidly applied in order to facilitate understanding. Of course, we might fail or be only partially understood but communication as the engagement in 'speech acts' between individuals presupposes agreement and mutuality. Speech acts are two sided and involve an 'utterer' and a 'hearer' who together create shared meaning. There are logical and semantic conventions inherent in communication and 'autonomy' is always constrained by these conventions in terms of 'how' things are said. The constraints on 'what' may be said are a mixture of the ethical, the political and contextually appropriate. Judgements on what is appropriate is thus a matter of shared judgement and a sensitive speaker is one who responds to his audience's reaction and is guided in what is uttered by the hearer's sense of appropriateness as well as his or her own. As learned skills, development of the ability to make judgements of this kind is a very relevant educational concern.

Limits to autonomy: the concept of intentionality

In discussing our ability to think as we choose, we are surely coming to the centre of what is meant by 'autonomy'. Our own thoughts must in some sense be the domain which others cannot reach? It might be accepted that we think in terms of learned language and that ordered sequencing as distinct from random thoughts is implied in the idea of 'thinking' and that we think to some purpose. It will be helpful therefore to consider the concept of 'intentionality', which is related to having purpose.

To behave or act with intention, or to intend that some state of affairs should obtain, seem to be criteria for 'autonomy' and they are central to our thinking about the nature of 'responsibility'. This concept, on which moral and legal thought depends is of practical and theoretical importance, and individuals are held responsible for actions and the consequences of actions which were intended. We might possibly be excused for behaving thoughtlessly or impulsively, but in most contexts, these terms are in stark contrast to rational behaviour which is almost a synonym of 'intentional' behaviour. 'Intentionality' as a concept hovers between theory and practice and we may say that 'intentions' govern practice.

A distinction may be made between the transitive verb form 'to intend that x' and the noun 'intentionality' as used philosophically to explain or account for the idea of 'consciousness' in our perception of the world. In this sense, perceived phenomena are not unmeditated 'sense data', 'sensations' or 'raw feels'. They are deemed to be preconceptualised objects which are 'seen as' examples of their kind. They are categorised in terms that have already been acquired and which have meaning and significance. 'Experience', following Husserl's argument for example, is an intentional relation, recognised and constructed by an experiencing self on the basis of previous experience.

We are said to have learned to make use of i.e. to have intentions to make use of experience as a means of extending our understanding each new phase of experience. 'Intentionality' as an instrumental purpose is built into the idea of consciousness itself. By definition, a 'conscious being' is an 'intentional being'. By imposing our consciousness upon the world, we are already making use of it and in this sense 'intentionality' is a pragmatic concept as embodied for example in William James' (1917) idea of 'the will to believe'. To summarise crudely, we can only 'see' something when we know what it is for and when we have a novel experience to try to make the best 'fit' in terms of existing language and conceptual schemes.

When we turn to decision making, Jane Heal (1990) distinguishes two related questions:
1)   What shall I do?
2)   What shall I intend?

Question 1) might be answered in moral terms thus converting it into a question about what 'I ought to do', or in terms of practical consequences without moral consequences (e.g. if I intend to keep dry, then I shall take an umbrella). In answering question 1) we begin to consider 2), the answers to which exemplify our intentions. We are therefore once more in the realm of having reasons which explain and justify our behaviour and choice of behaviour is a rationally made decision.

'Intention' may thus be seen as a mental concept which is essential to establishing the concept of 'agency' as when we refer to 'moral agents', 'freely chosen actions', 'personal decisions' and so on, all of which are related to 'autonomy'. They are constitutive and indicative of the state of 'being autonomous'.

In order to be absolutely autonomous and free 'to intend that p', an intention on the part of our autonomous action must be uncaused. Indeed the converse is required, namely that the agent shall be the cause, or the originator of his or her own intention, but this appears to produce an infinite regression. Why do

I intend what I intend . . ? A possible answer lies in the conception of 'reason' and 'rationality' but it might be argued that these provide *ex post facto* justifications for an action in which intention was manifest. 'Intention' itself is thus visualised as an uncaused cause as the concept of absolute autonomy requires, in which case reason giving is ruled out.

A different approach is to be found in Wittgenstein (1953, paragraphs 610 to 632) where he argues that some things are beyond the possibility of description because we lack an appropriate vocabulary. His example is the difficulty of describing an aroma where at best we rely on analogies as we noted when considering 'pains'. Similar difficulties occur when trying to define 'intentions' and 'acts of will'. Wittgenstein's solution is to evade the necessity for translation into a different but analogous vocabulary, and this he does by making 'intending' and 'willing' examples of a particular kind of language game. In saying "I am going to take two powders now and in half an hour I shall be sick" — it explains nothing to say that in the first case I am the (intending) agent and in the second merely the observer. By saying what I am going to do is the *expression* of my intention. It *is* my intention and in a similar way 'willing to raise my arm' is equivalent to 'raising my arm' not an action which precedes it. I might *decide* at which point in time to act but the *willing* is (expressed) in the action. No 'non-causal' bringing about is entailed. As Wittgenstein succinctly puts it (para.615) 'Willing, if it is not to be a sort of wishing, must be the action itself'.

The contingency of autonomy

These arguments bring out clearly a presupposition concerning 'autonomy' as 'intending', 'choosing' and 'deciding' and this is the presupposition that choices are contingent upon circumstances. An intention, a choice, must be contingently possible as well as logically possible. We are constrained by the facticity of the world and also by social constraints. In a very weak sense of the term, I might say 'I intend to go for a walk today' but this speech act need not imply that 'I will at all costs'. It might, quite correctly, from a linguistic point of view mean no more than 'I will if the opportunity arises' or 'I will if nothing more important prevents me'. Conditionality of this kind seems to be a more likely constraint.

The significance of these points in relation to our understanding of autonomy should now be clear. It is at most a constrained, regulated autonomy which can be attained. Even terms such as 'self-ruling', 'self-directing' and so on have contingently limited force, but we now move on to consider the logical impossibility of being 'self-ruling' in the light of a further set of Wittgenstein's arguments. In the absolute sense of the term an autonomous person should be capable of making his or her own rules, yet this seems to be an impossibility.

At this point, arguments from Wittgenstein (1953) and a related point made by Hampshire (1960) become relevant to understand what has been said. Hampshire's version may be paraphrased as follows:

Consider the question addressed to an agent 'what are you doing?' In order to know, the agent must be acting intentionally with a knowledge of both the nature and the purpose of whatever actions are being performed. In giving a reply there are several possibilities:

1)   The actions might be misdescribed
2)   The account of what is intended might be incorrect
3)   The answer 'I am not sure' is given
4)   Correct answers are given.

Unless genuine mistakes are made, the requirement of intentionality excludes all possibilities except 4). We must, logically must, know the correct answer in order to be deemed a responsible, autonomous agent. This follows from our understanding of 'intentionality'.

Wittgenstein's Thesis on Private Language and Rules

The starting point is his metaphor of 'language games' which include such linguistic activities as 'giving orders', 'describing', 'reporting', 'asking' and so on. Many possible moves might be made within a particular game but they are all governed by the rules implicit in that game. As with games such as chess or cricket, the games are defined by their rules and not to observe them is regarded as 'not playing (that) game'.

Similarly with language, understanding and demonstrating correct observance of its rules, makes one a competent linguist in respect of a given language. The question for Wittgenstein, taken up by Ayer (1956) and Kripke (1982) is whether it is possible to have a private language governed by private rules. The implications for 'personal autonomy' are considerable, where it is defined as 'self-ruling'.

Wittgenstein (1953 paragraphs 198 to 243) tries to demonstrate that it is logically necessary that at some point public rules are introduced.

In para 198 he asked '. . . how can a rule show me what I *have* to do at (a particular) point? Whatever I do is an interpretation in accord with the rule' but '. . . *whatever I do* (can) be brought in accord with the rule' (my italics). This conclusion follows, once the idea of `interpretation' is introduced.

The example of a signpost is then considered. Its finger points in a particular direction and I have learned that the correct interpretation of the sign is to walk in the direction indicated. Thus (para.202) 'correctly' obeying a sign is a matter of following a learned practice and so it is with the rules of language. They are a public matter.

But why can we not have private rules? Wittgenstein's reply is that '... to *think* one is obeying a rule is not to obey a rule. Hence it is not possible to obey a rule 'privately', otherwise thinking one was obeying a rule would be the same as obeying it'. To put the point the other way the possibility of behaving intentionally is removed because we could not know when we are doing what we intended to do. It is necessary to have a public reference in order to judge that we are actually doing what we thought we were doing. Otherwise we are prisoners in our solipsism.

It might now be objected that on this argument we cannot even know what our intentions are, but this only follows if intention is something that *can* be known. Wittgenstein then resorts to the analogy of private 'sensations', such as 'having a pain'. To claim honestly without intending to mislead that 'I have a pain' must tautologically be true. I cannot be mistaken. The concept of 'knowing' does not apply, because such self-referential statements are uniquely privileged. They must be true. A pain is a pain for me.

Similarly, my intentions cannot be doubted by me. If I consult other individuals, my autonomy is immediately compromised. On this view there-fore, 'intentionality' becomes a 'disposition'. I am predisposed towards 'that p'. I can say that '*I intend* "that p"' and grammatically the proposition is of the same form as 'I think "that p"'.

If 'that p' means 'following a rule' or a particular occasion, I can try saying 'I do think ...' or 'I am disposed to think ...' or 'I intend "that p"' (i.e. to follow a rule) and my autonomy seems absolute. However, in line with our argument above, *whatever* I think counts as following a rule will be correct, because I cannot judge what counts as being correct. I have no criteria by which to judge therefore the idea of 'correctness' has no place. I cannot judge sense from nonsense without reference points in an external world, therefore I need other people to help me judge my actions and my autonomy is again compromised.

This point is made in a different way by Wittgenstein (para. 265) by using the example of trying to remember the time of a train. This he says, cannot be done by trying to remember how the page of a timetable looked because no recollection in a sequence of recollections can guarantee the correctness of its predecessor. A memory is always fallible and a memory of a memory is likewise fallible, therefore the only valid check is to consult the timetable. To think that memory can be a check on memory is akin to consulting two identical copies of a newspaper to verify the truth of its news items.

Surely, a critic might say, this argument is counter-intuitive. I can understand a private rule such as 'I always rest every 15 minutes when digging my garden'. But this may be taken as a descriptive statement about what I do, and the rule is not separately articulated. My 'rule' *is* my observable behaviour, and 'rule' and 'action' are conflated. Does this matter? If a conceptual distinction has no force, ignore it.

What we do therefore, is to shift the concept of 'intention' from the mental, to the observable realm and 'intention' as a sign of 'mental autonomy' is translated from the form:

'I intend "that p"', into the form 'that p'.

Intention is manifest in its realisation, as when, say, an author writes a paper. Whether it is rational, rule governed and meaningful is a judgement about which the author cannot be sure. The distinction between 'believing that' and 'knowing that' has no function in the private domain. Judgements about meaning, rationality, significance, and so on can only be made in the public domain by knowledgeable and critical readers. What matters so far as autonomy is concerned is having freedom to make the attempt to communicate in various ways.

Conclusions

We can now draw the following conclusions:

1. The extent to which individuals are capable of thinking for themselves, and of making their own judgements, is a function of their mastery of a range of language games. These simultaneously constrain and enable. Mere babble is not language. Language consists of ordered disciplined sounds, or when written, of ordered disciplined use of signs and symbols. We can communicate by following recognised social practices, and the making of judgements may be thought of as the following of practices which are in turn recognised by others who share the same language. Just as 'intention' is manifest in its realisation, so are 'meanings' expressed in linguistic practices. Our intention to communicate and thereby to express or display our autonomy, is constrained by the necessity to follow accepted practices. If we do not (within limits) follow such practices there can be no communication, or at best, only incomplete communication. If, as we intend, we are to communicate we must do so on the recipient's terms.

This limits our autonomy but we have no option. Both parties to a communicative act are bound by the same rules and the same practices. Complete, unfettered autonomy is a myth and this is true of all our practices, whether linguistic or some other form of behaviour. If performed in public, our various practices must be publicly acceptable. We can engage in esoteric practices in private and thus try to maintain absolute autonomy but it would be an empty gesture. To engage in private practices in public, at a minimum produces misunderstanding and ridicule, or at worst ostracism or even punishment. We are once again on the boundary of 'autonomy' and 'sovereignty' as political concepts concerned with the regulation and containment of power.

The first conclusion can also be expressed in terms of Gadamer's (1975) hermeneutics, when he says (p.250) '. . . we always stand within a tradition which is not something alien. It is always a part of us . . .' We cannot escape from this tradition (although we might modify it) because it consists of practices as well as beliefs, or rather, as beliefs expressed in practices. These are manifest in the ways in which we behave. They have been acquired over many years and they form the background or *vorhahe* against which we function. Any novelty is influenced by what we already are and have learned to be. We start from a stance already acquired as part of a community within a network of overlapping communities. There is no *ab initio* self, neutral, autonomous and independent. The most that we can do is to follow public practices and make private use of public rules and public languages. In Wittgenstein's term (para.241) we function with a form of life defined by its social practices, and it is these which give us what we call 'autonomy'.

2.   Our second conclusion is that properly understood, adult education has a part to play, but it engages only indirectly in the development of personal autonomy. With the 'political' dimension education has no concern because it is powerless.   It can only provide the prerequisites for autonomy by introducing individuals to new skills knowledge and competencies which enable individuals to enlarge their range of practices. The powerlessness of adult educators should not be seen as a weakness, neither is it suggested that there is a moral or a political objection to them having a direct role in the development of autonomy. What is suggested, is that given the complex nature of what might be meant by 'autonomy', it is logically as well as contingently, not something that is teachable.   Within the limits already discussed, to be 'autonomous' is a status to be *acquired* and 'autonomy' is *exercised* by those who do not wish to move with the majority, but the majority has to agree. 'Autonomy' can therefore be a personal objective, indeed it has to be such otherwise we begin from a premise outside the individual which would be the obverse of autonomy. Individuals might not wish to carry the responsibility of autonomy therefore adult educators have no right to try to make it an educational objective on behalf of such individuals. Given the nature of the concept, 'autonomy' *per sé* is not in the category of educational objectives simply because it is not learnable but this conclusion does not exclude an adult education contribution to the learning of practices which indirectly help to make autonomy a possibility within the limits. Adult educators need to know what the limits of their responsibilities are, as well as knowing the limits to what they are capable of achieving.

In the end, it might be simpler to drop the idea of having 'autonomy' as an adult education objective and to concentrate instead on such objectives as helping adults to think and act in ways which indirectly might have a bearing on the achievement of individual autonomy while recognising the limitation of that concept.

Postscript

It might be objected that the preceding discussion assumes undue rigidity in the rules governing linguistic practices which is anachronistic in a pluralist culture as described by postmodernists. In response, it would be said that considerable flexibility in the interpretation of rules must always be allowed for. As in law, there will be 'penumbra' questions about the range of application of rules to cases. There will be differences of interpretation over meaning, extension of reference and so on. Linguistic invention will lead to misunderstanding and novelty will cause bewilderment. But if there are no rules, no criterial regulations, no agreements and conventions on the application of categories there can be no concepts such as 'correct' and 'incorrect' and without which there can be no discussion. It is also questionable whether there could be a concept of 'adult education'.

Footnote

In drawing the conclusion that 'identity' is explicable in conventional terms I am begging some very deep philosophical questions some of which are discussed by H. Putnam (1989) in an article entitled 'Convention: A Theme in Philosophy'. As in the above discussion and in Putnam's article on which I draw, Putnam contrasts 'convention' with the 'natural but not the latter with the 'unnatural'. I have attempted only to rely on 'conventionalism' in relation to a particular set of problems, not to present it as a general philosophical position. Nevertheless, this general position takes in the background as it inevitably must when a linguistic approach is adopted. As Putnam observes, 'For empiricism (the) "linguistic turn" meant a shift from psychologism to conventionalism'. The necessity of logical truths, and in the case of positivists, of mathematical truths as well was accounted for by saying that all of this was 'truth by convention'. We stipulate or legislate on what words mean. A similar view is implied in Wittgenstein's descriptions of 'language as practice' or the following of rules, a view of which ad hominem use is also made in the present article.

The dilemma posed by conventionalism is that 'stipulation' presupposes language, (as Quine had pointed out in 1936) which if it is rich enough to state generalisations and formulate convention in, uses logical words such as 'all, some, not, and, or, if, then' (a paraphrase of Putnam, 1989). Is logic therefore prior to convention as Quine said? Is logic just accepted as being incapable of further reduction? In answer to these kinds of question, Quine defined 'convention' as 'explicitly formulated rules' as contrasted with logic which in some sense is 'given'.

In a later book, D Lewis (1969) defined convention as a rule or a practice which is 'arbitrary' as when a decision is made to drive on the left, rather than the right side of the road. There is no 'logical' or 'natural' compulsion to do so and a decision is indeterminate.

By presenting my present paper largely in social, political and ethical, as well as in educational terms, these important issues are circumvented.

7
The concepts of 'tradition' and 'translation'

Introduction

Reference has been made in the earlier essays to the concept of tradition. We now try to relate the concept to language and the problem of translating 'meanings' between languages, and thereby understand what is being said by those working within other linguistic traditions. The problems are seen more clearly when dealing with languages such as English, French or German and between Western and Eastern languages embodying different cultural traditions. Similar problems arise however between subcultures nominally using the 'same' language (consider for example the alleged differences between 'middle-class' and 'working class' English). There are also similar problems when using technical languages using nonstandard vocabularies and in this sense 'academic subjects' are technical languages, representing particular intellectual traditions. 'Learning' can therefore be seen in part as learning to move between traditions and languages, and 'understanding' is in part a matter of translating the unknown into the known. This is a general educational problem but it can be seen as an issue in adult education at two levels.

Firstly, we are dealing with an issue relevant to multi-cultural societies, manifest in such adult education slogans as 'helping people to learn in the light of their own experience and in terms of their own questions'. Are they to be confined within existing subcultural discourse and if not, what is involved in translating unfamiliar codes, concepts and so on into their own terms?

Secondly, the same kinds of issue impinge upon the theorisation of 'adult education' and the ongoing debate about epistemological issues and the need to conceptualise adult education independently of existing disciplines and forms of knowledge while recognising its present interdisciplinary nature (see Barry P. Bright, ed. 1989). Here there is a merging of traditions and language with attendant problems of translation and interpretation and eventual synthesis. This essay tries to illustrate what is involved and the discussion continues in the final essay in relation to 'conceptual schemes'. The issues are within the following area, illustrated by a simple example.

The difficult concept of 'adult education' comes into the adult educators vocabulary from existing language and conceptual schemes. 'Adult' as Paterson (1979) demonstrates is a value laden status concept, developed within a liberal democratic tradition. 'Education' has a double connotation. It is 'liberating' yet also associated with 'schooling' which is a constraining concept. Two approaches to practice make use of the same signifier. How, that is to say, in what ways can tradition located concepts such as these be translated into a new idiom *and* continue to be understood from within the original language or discourse. To what extent does the 'new' concept escape from its roots within an allegedly new discourse? Griffin (in Bright 1979) illustrates new confusion when he says that 'Freire is concerned with education *as such*'. How can there be such a definitive category distinct from language, conceptual schemes and the interpretation and intentions of users?

The Importance of Tradition

Given that some of our central educational and social concepts such as 'truth', 'meaning', 'rationality' and so on, may be defined and explained in different ways, how might we decide on which version to accept and use? One possible answer is to say that the 'standard' version will be imposed by some power-wielding elite in a class based society. Another answer is to resort to 'tradition' but this too might be a suspect term with pejorative associations. 'Tradition' is however a useful concept which appears at a number of points both in these essays and in other literature. Some discussion of the concept might help to deepen our understanding and to clear the ground.

The term 'tradition' might suggest 'conservation' and unacceptable constraints imposed by the dead hand of the past, but a useful distinction can be drawn between 'traditional' or 'traditionalist' on the one hand, and 'tradition' as an ongoing and developing set of ideas on the other hand. A 'traditionalist', roughly speaking, might be someone who acts or performs repeatedly in similar ways on the grounds that some 'things have always been done that way'. Most of us are traditionalists in some way or other by e.g. celebrating festivals such as Christmas, Ramadan, Independence Day, or Bastille Day in familiar ways. I am a traditionalist in always writing with a pen or a pencil. But, festivals and ceremonies, such as the opening of Parliament are 'traditions' embodying some deeper meaning or significance. They have an ongoing purpose, although in the course of time they might lose support and fall into disuse. This could happen to the liberal tradition although it is very deeply rooted in what is called 'Western civilisation'. There are of course other deeply rooted traditions in the Middle East and Asia, as well as the relatively modern Marxist tradition which appears in various parts of the world. There are also sub-traditions in art, literature, music, sportsmanship and in philosophy each of which reflects to some extent the broader cultural tradition in which it appears.

It might be asked why traditions should be observed, and one answer is that they are inescapable even if used as a point of departure for the establishment of new traditions. The point has been made (e.g. Gombridge, 1966) that the history of art would be impossible had there not been particular artists at particular times, working within and developing 'styles' and as members of 'schools' each recognisable as such, yet different in some respects. Thus we speak of music in the 'classical' tradition, of 'French impressionist' and 'English landscape painters' and so on, each representing a tradition which provides as it were a 'vocabulary' which practitioners use and develop thus carrying on the tradition.

The metaphor of a 'vocabulary' in the arts becomes literal in linguistic practices in which concepts are developed and these enter into the discourse of politics, ethics and education and help to define a 'culture'. They help to give individuals and successive generations 'a voice' and in that sense the traditions embodied in the various discourses are liberating as well as constraining, a point referred to again in following essays. Even 'post-modernism', which might be seen as the outer limit of the liberal tradition, draws extensively upon the concept of 'individuality' and 'choice' but it tries to disassociate these ideas from social relations and make individuality 'free floating'. But this is impossible except in the relatively trivial areas which are wholly private and do not impinge upon the private spaces of other individuals. Even so, *ab initio* inventiveness which does not draw upon *some* tradition which provides its models is at most rare, and even new forms of say 'music' are still within a tradition of organised sound. 'Postmodern architecture' is eclectic in terms of style yet it draws upon architectural tradition.

The essential point to recognise, is that 'traditions' embody what in the broadest sense are vocabularies which are meaningful within a tradition although 'meaning' (discussed in Essay No. 8) is a difficult term to explain. 'To convey meaning' may be taken to imply that 'intention' is being expressed as when a command is given a question asked or an assertion made. 'Meaning as intention' may also be expressed in a 'design' as in say, a building designed to impress but it is difficult to visualise or comprehend 'intention' except within a tradition which recognises some degree of individual autonomy. In some cultures, and therefore in some traditions only 'Kings' have intentions, and slaves are deemed to have neither autonomy nor intention. In a democracy such terms have a very different connotation and a term such as 'justice' has a significance within a democratic or liberal tradition which is different from say 'the justice of God' in a theistic system such as Judaism. Words do more than refer and denote, they also carry evaluative and emotional overtones as do (or did) words such as 'empire', 'voluntary' and 'natural'. 'Meanings' in an extended sense, develop within a tradition of usage and we learn the 'force' of a term such as 'non-democratic' within a tradition which values democracy.

Are we locked into particular traditions?

'Educated' is a term with especially powerful connotations, as when contrasted with 'ill-educated', and 'education' in some contexts contrasts favourably with (an allegedly) lower status term such as 'training'. These are all tradition dependent accounts and 'education' may be regarded as a process for introducing newcomers to a tradition, or as might be the case with adults, aspects of a tradition that are less familiar. We talk of 'opening windows', 'consciousness raising' and so on as aspects and functions of adult education, a concept which is itself a part of a tradition.

It might be argued that to speak in the singular of 'a tradition' smacks of cultural imperialism but we must consider whether 'subcultures' in say a class based society, are discrete in all respects or only in some respects in relation to a major tradition. These seem to be questions eminently suited to a liberal adult education tradition which is then forced to reflect upon its own values. It is education as criticism and not only as 'initiation'. 'Cognitive values' are one criterion of a desirable educational tradition, but other values are also applicable. The values of 'expressiveness' 'inventiveness' of 'community', are all possible contenders for inclusion within an educational tradition as well as 'individuality', equality and autonomy.

The foregoing are all recognisable as 'liberal values', definitive of what is sometimes called an 'open society'. Associated with these values are ethical commitments. Is there any significant sense in which these can be translated into other traditions. How are they perceived from within other traditions?

The problem of translation

This major issue has been discussed by, for example, MacIntryre (1988), Davidson (1984), by Putnam (1983), Goodman (1977) and more obliquely by Quine, 1953). The 'problem of translation' raises questions about how, and to what extent translation is possible between traditions, and also between languages. It is perhaps more accurate to say that two issues are involved rather than one because languages may be seen in part as constituting a tradition and also as features within a tradition. As constitutive of a tradition they are also carriers of that tradition. They embody or possess its distinctive values and conceptual schemes. From within the tradition, defined as a set of practices languages portray the tradition. In the latter sense, a tradition such as the liberal tradition might be portrayed or expressed in say, English, French, German and

Danish. But if this is the case, each language must be translatable into the others, and this requires common or compatible conceptual schemes which are merely expressed in different words which are synonyms as in the case of say 'snow' and 'schnee', in English and German respectively. But some words are not literally translatable in this way as in the case of the German 'Erwachsenbildung' sometimes used as an equivalent of 'adult education' which German speakers have difficulty in explaining in English. Mere word substitution clearly is not the whole of what is meant by 'translation'. A complex of values and ideas has to be conveyed.

The problem is thus transferred to definitions of 'traditions' as embodied in more than one language, if by 'tradition' we mean in part at least that it embodies values and concepts. But if concepts and values are embedded in languages which are not exactly similar, in what sense do they embody the same tradition? This might appear to be an esoteric question but it raises educational issues and questions about the way in which particular traditions are described and defined and about the meanings attached to the word 'tradition' itself as a universal term. The problem also appears, perhaps more importantly in trying to teach say 'Marxism' from within the 'liberal tradition' or vice-versa. In addition, there is the problem that competing social and philosophical positions were formulated in different natural languages. An example which I have difficulty with is the Marxists' use of the word 'praxis' which is not an English word and it is used as a technical term which represents a 'concept', understandable in the context of a total theory. Another example is the 'dialectic' which has Aristotelian roots, but within Marxist theory has changed its meaning. On the liberal side, the concept of 'rights' might create difficulties for those within other traditions, and other languages, simply because it is a part of a total conceptual scheme with a particular history.

For the time being the concept of 'tradition' will be left on one side in favour of a discussion about the problem of translation between natural languages as the prior issue.

One obvious problem is that in order to translate say the word 'schnee' into 'snow' we have to recognise what it means in German in order to match it with a word of similar meaning in English. We are required to understand or to know what 'schnee' means in order to make the translation. The difficulties are multiplied in more complex phrases, especially when dealing with obtuse subjects. In such cases, the meaning of individual words is of little use and it is their use in sentences, and moreover, sentences within a total discourse which have to be understood. Complete understanding is demonstrated when new and unforeseen sentences can be understood and generated. If speaker's intentions are recognised as generating meaning it is apparent that 'translation' is a complex matter and use must be made of 'interpretation' which is also complex. As Davidson (1984) points out use is made of 'indexical devices' such as 'tense' to make truth claims within a language, 'relative to a time and a speaker'. He therefore concludes that a theory of truth for a language is essential to the understanding of a language.

This, he argues, enables us to understand when words are correctly applied, a view recently criticised by Hacker (1996) who says that 'like Quine, Davidson leaves no room for explanation of meaning, for asking what a word means and being given explanations. He assumes without warrant that coming to understand an alien language *begins* (my italics) with what he calls assigning "truth conditions" to sentences "held true"'. Hacker's point is the obvious one that language consists of more than the making of true assertions. Questions are asked, orders are given and intentions are conveyed. Nevertheless, when we are dealing with assertorial sentences, where reference is to some simple observation as in the case of sentences referring to observable natural kind categories such as 'snow', 'rain' and so on in which ostensive definition is possible, translation is still relatively simple. It is with abstract notions such as 'the dialectic' and similar theoretical terms that the problems emerge. What do such terms describe? To what do they refer? What makes their assertion true?

To return to the problem of understanding Marxism (this example is not intended to denigrate Marx), what might be made of 'the dialectic' by an unfamiliar adult education class. Consider the example from Allman and Wallis (1995). Speaking of Gramsci, they say:

'It is also fairly certain that he recognised the difference between Marx's dialectic and that of Hegel — a difference that goes beyond the reversal of idealism. Marx's dialectic was a concrete method grounded in material reality ... Marx began from the assumption that capitalist reality (and in different ways all hitherto real worlds) was founded on dialectic contradictions'.

As a teaching problem involving 'translation' into a language understandable to students, the difficulties seem to be considerable. A considerable amount of background knowledge has to be understood and the idea of 'dialectical contradictions' has to be convincingly demonstrated as well as theoretically restated in various ways. In particular, Marx's assumption has to be placed in relation to the philosophy of Hegel and his concept of the 'Doppelsatz' translated into English as 'double dictum'. This dictum was itself formulated in two ways thus requiring two English translations and at least two interpretations. The concept of a 'dialectical logic' has different meanings in Hegel's and Marx's philosophy and in English the term 'dialectic', as has been noted, has connotations from Aristotle. This illustrates the complexity of translation between traditions. It also supports Hacker's point that more is required than Davidson's 'assignment of truth-conditions to sentences'. In philosophical terms the truth-conditions for 'the correct application require definition and demonstration'. No doubt there are strategies for coping with the problems inherent in teaching such ideas and my present purpose lies in demonstrating some of the complexities at a philosophical level that have to be faced by all teachers. What such strategies require are both truth conditions and the conditions of rational acceptability appropriate to various kinds of assertion, as interpreted from within a language which is not the original.

In conclusion of this introductory survey we return to the concept of 'traditions' as distinct from 'languages' where similar issues arise. The first point worth noting, is the narrowness of the distinction drawn between 'languages' and 'traditions' because in an obvious sense, a 'tradition' (as we noted above) is defined by its practices of which its linguistic practices or modes of discourse are probably the most important.

Conclusion

MacIntyre (1988), who adopts an historical approach, starts from an assumption similar to the one made above, namely that in order to understand and translate rival and competing traditions, a precondition is that there should be a significant measure of mutual understanding. This, in his view is '... sometimes to be achieved only by a set of historical transformations; either, or both of the traditions may have had to enrich itself significantly in order to provide a representation of some of the characteristic positions of the other, and this enrichment will have involved both conceptual and linguistic innovation and quite possibly social innovation too.' This contrasts sharply with the a-temporal or timeless approach of some of the writers such as those mentioned earlier.

MacIntryre's view requires that adherents of competing traditions can be understood as having modes of thought, beliefs and values that are not radically different. This ensures some compatibility between views on what counts as rational acceptability. But this view appears to put both traditions within some broader tradition. It does not allow for what might be called 'radical difference'.

In the tradition of say Davidson, Putnam and Quine, a shared semantics is postulated and semantic analysis is seen as providing a foundation on which to make comparisons and translations possible. Language *per se* is the shared tradition, and translation, at least in part, consists in identifying 'same saying' in different versions of language. 'Snow is white' and 'schnee ist weiss' are examples of same-saying.

MacIntyre in effect merges the semantic and the historical approaches by regarding the evolution of modern liberalism as a dual process of same-saying and linguistic innovation through Greek and Latin, into which the Greek language introduced a previously absent philosophical tradition. He observed also, that in Cicero's Rome, 'there was no way to discuss political matters . . .

except within a framework supplied by the standard uses of '*republica*', '*auctoritas*', '*dignitas*', '*libertas*', '*imperium*' and the like'.

Similar observations might be made of the current liberal democratic framework of 'individuality', 'rights', 'justice' and 'equality' which governs much political discussion, or on the Marxist side, 'class', 'oppression', 'revolution', 'legitimacy' and so on are a staple in the discussion of politics. The ensuing process of translation between traditions takes place in linguistic communities which in hermeneutic fashion view the past and each other, in terms of their current interpretation of the present, coloured by interpretations of the past. Thus the Marxists view current problems in the light of a theory of history which is not neutral, because that theory has been formulated in order to illuminate the problems of the present and to validate action in the future. Liberals do likewise within their own theories of history which determine what is selected as historically relevant in the past.

8

Rationality, meaning and truth

Introduction
A foundational concept

The concept of 'rationality' is deeply embedded in liberal democratic cultures where it can be seen as one of a group of regulatory ideas and practices alongside 'morality' and 'law'. These can all be called 'institutional' or 'institutionalised' concepts in the sense that their values and practices, their rules and procedures are all publicly validated. 'Rationality' may also be regarded as foundational in that it provides or specifies, normative principles which define what is meant by 'rules' and 'procedures', and to that extent, 'law' and 'morality' are derived from the idea of 'rationality'. The latter is also regarded in some traditions, of which the liberal traditional is one, as a defining characteristic of a developed human being, and this explains why the development of 'rationality' has become an educational aim. This is my justification for introducing a subject once more. It is an already much discussed subject and therefore there is considerable disagreement on what it means.

What is intended here, in what can only be an outline account is to introduce to those engaged in the education of adults, a number of ideas and sources with which they might not be familiar. The content however, is not specific to adult education. A further intention is to try to demonstrate that 'rationality' is not an optional extra, but an idea built into the practices of language and thought. It is therefore a socially necessary concept, and a logically necessary concept without which I could not be writing this essay, neither would any reader comprehend it. The importance to education of the idea of rationality seems to be self-evident. It does not follow that there is only one form of 'rationality' or one theoretical explanation and these are matters on which there is ample scope for disagreement.

At an everyday level, the main outlines might be simply expressed. Most of us know how and when to judge that someone has acted irrationally. We can understand what it means to think rationally and we have a capacity to do so in an everyday sense. This is a crucial point to grasp because it illustrates the embeddedness of 'rationality' as a 'commonsense' practice. The concept of 'understanding' is also fundamental. We can understand (or learn to do so) language, arguments, situations, instructions, commands, requests and so on and 'understanding' can be explained partly in terms of 'meanings' as interpretations. All of this is possible because of the articulation in consistent ways of 'sounds', 'gestures', 'signs' and 'symbols' embodied in what we call 'thought' and 'language'. What we call 'communicative rationality' is, in varying degrees, tacitly understood and practised from an early age.

A distinction may be made between 'practical' and 'communicative' rationality, although the two ideas overlap, and we engage in the former when making decisions on how to act, when solving problems and diagnosing faults in a 'system' whether it be mechanical, administrative or biological. The distinction between 'thought' and 'action' in such contexts is blurred and a useful discussion may be found in Ryle (1947). But we might look a little more closely at the idea of rational action, to which we now turn.

Rational Action

This is rather an ambiguous idea, but one criterion of rational action is that it be done with intent. We try, or intend to achieve some purpose, and then work out a strategy designed to fulfil or realise our intent. This presupposes the possibility of judging the consequences, or probable consequences of doing one thing rather than another. This in turn assumes the possibility of establishing which of several possible consequences realises the intention. In everyday situations, we employ informal logic using logical connectives such as 'if', 'then' and 'therefore'.

A simple example would be the process of arriving at a decision on how to travel from 'A' to 'B' in the shortest time and at least cost. There might be three options available; to travel by train, bus or car. Timetables and journey times, and relative costs are known; and a direct comparison produces a determinate solution only if we can weight the desirable 'shortest time' and 'least cost'. We might not be able to realise both, but once 'intention' is sufficiently refined to either 'time' or 'cost' criteria the solution is obvious. The rationality of the deliberation drives not from the rightness or sophistication of the logic but in the clarity of purpose or intent. The essential point however, is not that a chain of syllogistic or any other logical reasoning has been carried out. It is only required that reasons, as 'justifications' can be provided. The logic is implicit in the way that 'grammar' is implicit in everyday speech.

We may say provisionally that 'rationality' is not directly associated with formal logic but with the giving of 'reasons' as a justification for an action and as a demonstration of consistency and compatibility between actions and outcomes.

In many situations, standard or conventional solutions are available and the same specification will be given to anyone asking a question of the same type. To the question 'what is the quickest way into town?' asked at a particular location, the answer might be 'take a number three bus at the corner of this street'. Not to take such advice could be regarded as irrational, or in more popular language, simply foolish. But to make it rational in a more strict sense, we need to know that the informant is reliable and this requires the making of a judgement based on criteria beyond the specific dialogue. To be rational therefore requires that we decide on assumptions about certainty or high probability, which in turn is recognised as a reasonable thing to do.

In a variety of situations, especially in the fields of technology and science, standard procedures, and tested theories are taken as guides to action and most cultures are likely to have paradigms of rational acceptability and here there are parallels with moral reasoning where some actions are always prima facie moral actions, thus 'truth telling' is expected in all but a few exceptional circumstances in which counter principles might seem appropriate. In liberal theory and in liberal societies, the pursuit of self-interest is usually regarded as a standard example of rational action although counter arguments might be given in some contexts, where the 'public interest' for example seems to have justified priority. Value judgements and rational judgements overlap and the rationality of particular outcomes is used as a criterion for judging 'intentions'. 'Rationality' thus becomes a normative concept which defines what is acceptable and approved in societies which try to avoid detailed specifications of the 'good'. But why is 'rationality' per se so highly valued?

MacIntyre (1988) argues that rationality has a history and that there are competing rationalities, each of which 'is inseparable from the intellectual and social tradition in which it is embodied, having emerged from, and as a part of a history of enquiry'. He goes on to say: 'Those who construct theories within such a tradition of enquiry and justification, often provide theories with a structure in terms of which certain theses have the status of first principles ... but what justifies the first principles themselves, or rather the whole structure of which they are a part is the *rational superiority* of that particular structure to all other attempts', (my italics). This is what is meant by 'institutionalised rationality'. Its standards are set by social institutions, of which 'education' is one example, and 'service' is another. The concept of 'rational superiority' appears to be lifting itself by its own bootstraps in that 'rationality' is its own judge and the idea of 'progress' is entailed.

Although 'rationality' is described as a 'regulatory' concept, and thus as a constraint, it is regarded by liberal theorists as a liberating concept. It empowers those who follow rational principles and procedures by diminishing the elements of chance and contingency and freeing individuals from the constraints of norms which define 'the good' in absolute terms as in say religious systems and political ideologies. There is freedom under a social system which values rationality, which should be seen in much broader terms than the application of rules of logic and the following of standard algorithms. As MacIntyre rightly observes 'the laws of logic are only a necessary, not a sufficient condition for rationality'. He also provides a number of historically developed additional criteria which include:

1)   action based on the calculation of costs and benefits to oneself as a possible consequence of an action.

2)   action under those constraints of impartiality which accord no particular privileges to ones own interests.

3)   action intended to achieve the ultimate and true good of human beings.

A variety of political, religious and ethical positions is possible and in the absence of 'meta-rational' criteria, ideological criteria rule out in advance some options. Attempts such as 'logical positivism' to provide a scientific basis for rationality have not succeeded and a useful discussion is to be found in Putnam (1981). Briefly, the aim was to produce what he describes as a scientific method based on the notion of 'verification', as the basis of a theory of meaning which would provide a 'list or canon' of 'what is and what is not a cognitively meaningful statement'. This canon embraces all rational statements and 'exhausts rationality itself' by comprehensively defining it. In the absence of success with this project, we are left with 'institutionalised rationality', and the possibility of pluralism in rational principles. A counter argument would be that logic in both necessary and sufficient but 'logic' is not a unitary concept. There is a variety of logics including formal, divided into inductive and deductive, the mathematical logics of Frege and Bool, symbolic logic, and truth functional logic.

However rationality is described we might still agree with Schick (1984) that 'rationality is also a concept which helps to define ourselves' and in identifying the concept of rationality implicit in a culture, we display something of ourselves and we might not like what we see. MacIntyre shows how the 'outcome centred' view of rationality comes out most clearly in modern liberal thinking where in recent years, the desired outcome 'has been reduced to the single initial premise expressed in the form 'I want it to be the case that such and such'. If taken literally, any personal want, however trivial is deemed 'rational' and the expression of personal preferences and the making of choices is a rational action. In other words, it is an 'anything goes' view of rationality which diminishes the concept of rationality because the premise is ultimately non-rational. This might imply of course, that human beings are ultimately non-rational and self-centred. On the other hand a minimal rationality is implied in satisfying a want.

The Rationality of Choice

Rawls (1982) puts forward a closely argued case for a rationality based on choice, which might be regarded as being ethically and rationally superior to a self-centred rationality of 'wants'. He seeks presuppositions on which social institutions are based and tries to secure a rational foundation for society itself. His thesis is that if it can be shown that a single principle can be agreed upon, then it will be rational to act in ways which support the principle. This is sound reasoning, but Rawls asserts rather than argues that 'Justice is the first virtue of institutions, as truth is to systems of thought'. 'Justice' which historically has been defined in a number of ways, is defined as 'fairness' in Rawls' system and he regards it as necessary to the existence of a good society. It has a function, but it is also an ethical value based on the premise that a 'just' or 'fair' society is a good society, although this premise can be taken back to the pragmatic principle that such a society is the only one which works.

A rationality based upon fairness is intended to secure cooperation between disparate individuals who already value the ability to make free choices. The society which binds them together must therefore be a consequence of their combined choices expressed as a social contract established in one joint act, which 'assigns rights and duties' and 'determines the divisions of social benefits' on a fair basis. 'Mutual cooperation' effectively becomes the most rational way forward because it supports the self-interest of individual members of a society who have agreed to accept constraints. An ethical and political rationality is accepted, and it embodies J S. Mill's conception of a 'beneficent liberalism' which respects individuality but does not create a morality of 'individualism'.

Rule Based Rationality

'Rationality' might also be expressed as a belief in 'rule governance' and the practice of 'rule invoking'. Black (1967) expounds the rule invoking argument as a way of justifying actions and of explaining what is meant by 'rational thinking'. We need not consciously follow rules which are implicitly being followed in action, thought and speech, but if called upon to do so, what we do can be explained and justified by invoking the implicit rules being observed. 'Rationality' is now defined as a system of rules and it plays a part in the discourse of 'justification'. There is an assumption that as social beings, we should be prepared at any time to justify what we are doing in ways which go beyond the expression of personal wants and preferences. 'Rationality as reason' and 'reasoning' becomes a process of 'giving reasons' or at least being committed to doing so if called upon. The notion of 'responsibility' is also implied as a concept which has meaning in a context which depends upon actions being planned and intentional. We are not held responsible for what is beyond our control, and rationality is a means for demonstrating control and intention.

In the 'rule invoking' mode, rules are a justification, and in following rules, they act as a guide. In accepting rules, they are a form of governance, they have 'authority'. They represent 'good ways' to approach stated objectives and when embodied in rational arguments and trains of thought, rule following helps to define and redefine objectives. They demonstrate hitherto unforeseen ways forward by indicating the most rational options. Thus an adult education class might wish to study a contemporary issue and by considering the evidence and evaluating it, the class reasons its way to the conclusion that they ought to begin with the historical origins thus converting say, a contemporary political issue into an historical one. Rationality in this sense widens horizons as well as constraining them at some points. In fact rules in the minimal sense of grammatical rules which make languages possible, are indispensable. In order to judge a situation, to distinguish between what is regarded as 'right' or 'wrong', 'correct' or 'incorrect' and so on are procedural rules and criteria which are seen most clearly in the domain of law and science but also in ideological systems of thought such as e.g. 'liberalism' and 'Marxism'. These are examples of 'institutionalised' norms and as a group, they may be described as 'criterial conceptions of rationality' (Putman, 1981).

Scientific rationality and the historical dimension

Scientific rationality, as Popper (1952) expresses it, is exemplified when 'theorist or experimenter puts forward statements or systems of statements and tests them step by step. In the field of the empirical sciences more particularly, he constructs hypotheses, or systems of theories and tests them against experience by observation and experiment'. On his view, theories are never proved, but their propositions may be falsified by counter evidence produced by researchers. Practical scientists, in my experience, however claim that theories are judged by their results. The test is 'do they work' and on this criterion, some theories are good and others are poor. They are neither proved nor falsified but they might fall into disuse and be replaced by others. In this form, we are facing a problem which has already been referred to above concerning the identification of 'superior rationalities'. The practical working scientists' tests are pragmatic. Results count as criteria and this might be accepted as one more example of a rational criterion. Kuhn (1962 and 1970) agrees with Popper on many issues but claims that Popper (and working scientists who are not philosophers) is only correct in his description of what scientists do when working in 'normal' science within existing paradigms. When judging between paradigms, or defining new ones, scientists make what Kuhn describes as 'gestalt' or intuitive shifts which are extra-rational. Again we have a variant on the general philosophical puzzle of judging when to change paradigms and invent or accept new 'criterial rationalities'. How do the various communities 'license' new rationalities and new criterial paradigms?

It is important to note that in what he calls normal science, 'puzzle solving' is being carried out, not the testing of theories in Popper's sense and it might be said that in everyday life existing paradigms of rationality are used to confront the puzzles of everyday life. I define 'puzzle' here as having a determinate solution in contrast to 'problems' which might have no solution (e.g. 'the problem of poverty'). When puzzles become problems that is to say, when existing rationalities and procedures prove to be inadequate it would seem that the rational thing to do would be to develop new rationalities, and this I believe is what MacIntyre is describing in 'Whose Justice? Which Rationality?'. His thesis, it will be remembered, is that 'rationality itself, whether theoretical or practical, is a concept with a history and this is in sharp contrast to 'enlightenment rationality' seen as a system of timeless truths. Because rationality may be seen as radical historically, each new epoch (or however history is divided) is still within the same historical tradition and this itself is a perceived interpretation rather than as an objective 'natural kind' process. For MacIntyre, a rational person is located historically and all rational persons anywhere in the world, will understand (or could learn to understand) the development of their tradition which evolves and produces new paradigms as new puzzles arise. This might be stretching MacIntyre's argument but it does not seem to exclude intuitive insights and gestalt leaps if these are seen within the context of a shared language. Indeed MacIntyre states that 'what a particular doctrine claims is always a matter of the linguistic particularities of its formulation ...'. Some of the criticism of Kuhn seems to follow a similar theme, but these are beyond our immediate concern. The point that I wish to make is twofold: exploration, development and invention which embody imaginative leaps are all rational activities and processes which at each stage require and may be given, justified assent before entering the extended canon. Secondly, language is the embodiment of such canon and it is the inherent rationality of language as the most important human characteristic which we shall discuss in the next section. Before doing so however, brief reference might be made to the possibility of being accused of confining thought and expression within the limits of a particular language and therefore implying support for the theses of radical relativism. Kuhn (1970) hints at this possibility when he refers to the difficulty of communicating across the boundaries of scientific specialities, and elsewhere (1962) he puts forward the 'incommensurability thesis' that terms used in another culture or historical period cannot be equated with meaning and reference in ours. 'Scientists with different paradigms inherit different worlds'. Putnam's 'knockdown' refutation must for the moment suffice, when he observes that Kuhn and Feyerabend 'tell us that Galileo had incommensurable notions and then go on to describe them at length' and this 'is totally incoherent'.

Intention, Meaning and Communication

Language appears to be a paradigm of a rational system, and communication a paradigm rational activity, yet both language and rationality are partly premised on a psychological notion.

It is a feature of the concept of 'rational action' that it be performed with intent. An accidental action might contingently turn out to have been 'the rational thing to do' but this is nonstandard usage. With language, it can be argued that it must be intentionally used if communication is to take place and meaning conveyed with some degree of accuracy. This involves the observance of a series of rules - grammatical, semantic and syntactic, although as with other forms of rational activity the rules may be implicit and to be able to follow these is part of what is meant by understanding a language.

The following account, which covers only a very narrow range of the very extensive debate about meaning, is meant only to be illustrative. The examples chosen have this purpose in mind and I wish to show how language has rules and convention embedded in it and by definition is a rational activity. The thesis being demonstrated is that communication is impossible unless a number of criteria are satisfied and in setting these out, a theory of meaning is implied. The first criterion is 'intention' as a starting point from which to explain 'meaning' and it places 'communication' within the category of 'actions' where 'intention' is a criterion of 'rationality'.

Communication is not necessarily linguistic. It can be carried out by using flag signals, gestures and tones of voice as an example based upon Grice (1957) illustrates. He argues that when making an intended meaning clear to a second party we are trying to establish a belief in the second party's mind. Thus a swimmer in danger of being swept out to sea on an outgoing tide is likely to shout and possibly wave an arm. These actions might be and sometimes are misunderstood and an onlooker could simply wave in return on the assumption that the swimmer was enjoying an experience. His intention however is to make watchers onshore believe that he, the swimmer, is in danger and is in need of assistance. The 'meaning' expressed is the swimmers intention. The meaning as interpreted by the onlooker is what the signals mean to him. The signals have to be 'read' and their meaning is manifest in their use as in a Wittgensteinian 'language game' which assumes the understanding and observance of a number of conventions. The participants must know the rules in order to understand each other. Grice therefore introduces two key notions (1) utterers' meaning and (2) hearers' or audiences' meaning. The problem lies in making the two coincide, and the procedures implicit in the act of communication might be set out as follows.

This example is from Grice (1975) illustrating the 'logic' of what he calls 'assertorial communication'. The italics are mine.

'By uttering 'I'm blue' Jones means that he is sad, if and only if Jones utters 'I'm blue' *intending:*

1)   that his audience *believes* that he is sad;
2)   that the audience *recognises* his intention (1);
3)   that this recognition be part of the audience's *reason* for believing that he is sad'.

Utterers' intention (a rational criterion) together with the audience's recognition of that instruction are each crucial to the transmission of meaning. This is conveyed in words chosen as the vehicle of the utterers' intention, but as conventional symbols and sounds with dictionary type meanings attached to them, their communicative meaning is generated contextually in the way in which the words are used. This is Wittgenstein's notion embedded in his metaphor of 'language games' in which participants are aware of the rules.

Saying and implying

Grice (1968) drew attention to the importance of the 'distinction between what the speaker said and what he has "implicated"'. Grice also distinguished between:

1)   'indicative type utterances' which convey the intention that the audience should come to believe something, and
2)   'imperative type utterances' such as 'commands' which convey the intention that the audience should do something. But, and I am not sure that Grice recognises this, there appear to be circumstances in which the 'indicative' and the 'imperative' conflate, but this point is valid only if a position similar to Ryle's (1947) is adopted, which regards 'thinking' as a form of 'doing' and regarding 'believing' as a form of 'thinking'.

'Believing', however might also be regarded more passively as a state of mind, the latter being a psychological concept. On the distinction between 'thinking' and 'believing', dictionaries give examples, and counter examples on each side of the argument. This illustrates the ambiguity inherent in language which cannot be wholly regimented, nevertheless an element of discipline is necessary 'in order to minimise understanding'. Inventive and imaginative usage is present in literary and poetic language, and to a more limited extent in everyday communication where meaning is flexibly created. But there are limits if language is to function as communication. The signals have to be understandable and understood and these requirements depend upon consistency and rule governance to a considerable extent. Grice expresses this requirement in unstructured type utterances such as 'hand waving' and in structured type utterances expressed sententially. The utterer reasons to the conclusion that a particular utterance is an effective way of getting an audience to believe what is intended by reasoning from the same premise. Such language should of course be taken as an analysis and an explanation of what takes place. It is not a step by step description of what goes on in the minds of the speakers and listeners.

In making a distinction between what is 'said' and what is 'implicated' problems are raised which have been hinted at but not explored. Two separate issues have been involved. Firstly, indicative statements which refer to what is the case. In the example of our swimmer who signals that he is drowning by shouting and waving, draws attention to what an onlooker might see, but not comprehend, namely a figure in the water making oral and visual gestures. The signals convey two 'messages'. One is the proposition 'I am drowning' which is clearly separate from the signal which expresses it. The proposition states 'the facts of the case' but in this example they are not verbalised. The observer is left to make an interpretation of the situation using only visual clues to identify the proposition 'I am drowning' or from the observer's point of view 'a man is drowning'. The situation is indeterminate and as we have suggested can be wrongly interpreted. 'Proposition' therefore seems to be founded on 'reality', or what is observable yet the expression of the proposition in language (which might be silently expressed as 'thoughts') has to be applied. Rules or at least 'guidelines' are necessary.

The drowning man is however making two simultaneous utterances. He is also signalling 'do something' and this is an 'imperative' or 'command'. When imperatives are expressed linguistically, they are distinguished from indicative assertions of 'fact' by the grammatical device of 'mood'. 'Do x' embodies the implied subjunctive 'you should do x' and the person to whom the order is given understands this and therefore has reasons for obeying, provided that the legitimacy or authority of the 'should' is accepted. The response, to obey or not to obey is dependent upon acceptance of what is implied in an accompanying proposition implicit in the command or order. The imperative 'do' is justified by 'because you should' (or 'ought' or 'must'). We are moving into moral language in which the status of terms such as 'should', 'ought' and 'must' is a source of contention and disagreement. Are they embedded in propositions or what? Nevertheless, in terms of communication, the use of the subjunctive mood indicates a prima facie rule to be observed, and once again, context indicates whether a paradigm case is one to act upon. Normally we do not argue about whether or not we go to the rescue of a drowning person. Understanding and response go together provided that two conditions are satisfied:

1)   That the 'signals' are genuinely and honestly made.
2)   We assume the truth of the matter.

Grice has pointed out that in addition to what has just been said 'truth' enters into the imperative case in a different way. The intention behind the imperative e.g. 'close the door' is to make it true that the 'door is closed', and the 'door is closed' is a proposition. Connections are once more being made between language and reality and it might be asked what makes it a true proposition that 'the door is closed'. Imperative and indicatives move closer together and concepts of 'truth' are involved as a component in understanding meaning.

Truth and Meaning

If someone says 'do x' a natural response might be 'why?'. If someone says 'x is the case' a response might be 'is that true?'. The 'why' question elicits a reply in the form of a justificatory explanation, or a reasoned argument, of which it might be asked is it 'valid' or 'is it correctly argued?'. All this suggests that a family of related terms is being used and that 'truth', 'true', 'valid', 'correctly reasoned' and 'justified' are members. This makes the 'problem of truth' more tractable by taking it out of the realm of metaphysical speculation about truth with a capital 'T' and locating it along with other linguistic terms explicable in terms of how they are used. In making this move, it helps to demonstrate the incomprehensibility of some current claims that there is no agreed truth, and the related claim that there is no objective knowledge. The obvious response is that if there is no truth, neither claim can be true and that in asserting such claims, concepts of truth are already presupposed.

By adopting an approach based on linguistic usage we are attempting in a rational way to make sense of what we actually say when using the terms 'is true' and 'the truth' in ordinary sentences and utterances. We are also asking why we use them, and one answer is that they provide assurance, and justification among other things. In accepting a claim 'as true' it becomes rational to act on the strength of such a claim. It is rationally justifiable to act on a 'truth claim', and 'rationality' and 'truth' are seen as interdependent notions. They have value as well as meaning, or rather they can be used in a meaningful way. As Putnam (1981) puts it 'rationally acceptable' and 'true' are notions that take in each others washing, they form part of a linguistic system which is logically articulated. Putnam further argues that 'being rational involves having criteria of relevance' and that 'a being with no values would have no facts either'. A 'factual claim' is a 'truth claim' and a 'rationally relevant claim' and as such a linguistic anchor.

Such arguments might seem to commit us to some form of relativism in which 'context' is a significant concept. Putnam allows this claim by referring to Dewey's point that 'some values are rational given the circumstances' but the other half of this assertion is that 'some values are objectively relative, i.e. rational and warranted in (an) actual existential setting'.

Putnam also argues 'The decision that a picture of the world is true (or true by our present lights or as "true" as anything is) answers the relevant questions (as well as we are able to answer them)'. We take it as 'true' for example that we are all constrained by the values, concepts and grammar actually available to us and it is this 'fact' which constitutes the ways in which we constitute ourselves. As individuals we are not solipsists (I believe that other people exist) and we are members of linguistic and other types of communities. There are problems of indeterminacy of interpretation (see Quine, 1951) but we do translate with varying degrees of success and Quine makes considerable use of the notion of 'probability' rather than 'certainty within the context of general theories about the world'. This is roughly the view of scientists who, within theories accord probability weightings to a range of confirming and informing instances, relevant to particular statements. A similar view is implied in logical positivism and for Ayer (1956) to claim 'to know' was to claim the 'right to be sure'.

The idea of a general theory about the world as a necessary condition for the generation of meaning and truth, is echoed in a different way by Davidson (1984). He states categorically as a self-evident truth that 'in sharing a language, in whatever sense this is required for communication, we share a picture of the world that must in its large features be true'. He also asks how we can understand each other, make sense of differences as between 'right' and 'wrong' other than 'against a background of shared belief'. There is ample justification for such a view in the way that most people believe in and accept a view of the experienced world in which we can make plans, do things, explain things with a reasonable assurance of success. We 'know' that if we go out in the rain we will get wet unless we wear a waterproof, we know enough about the world to make things, grow things and so on, and Davidson is surely right in postulating community of belief over a wide range of experience and over most of the world. This too makes nonsense of postmodern claims that no one now has a belief in grand narratives. It is only some kinds of narrative that are out of fashion, and in Davidson's terminology 'beliefs are identified and described within a dense pattern of beliefs'. This is an holistic theory and moreover, one which fits any culture. What Davidson is attempting is to set out the preconditions for any conceptual scheme in any language, which in order to function as a language must logically have some sentences which refer successfully and thus be 'valid' or 'true'. Only then does it become possible to assert what is false or 'incorrect' and for relativists to argue their case because that case itself requires that it is possible to understand other languages and other cultures in order to advance the claim that they are different.

This case is well expressed by Norris (1988) when he says of cultural relativists for whom 'meaning is entirely a matter of social convention . . . no means could possibly exist for translating observation sentences from one language to another. And the same would apply to Foucault's idea that truth is nothing more than a reflex product of discursive power relationships, a value attached to certain forms of utterance that currently enjoy that status'. If we cannot distinguish the true from the false, '. . . the relativist would be in the untenable position of asserting it as a generalised truth about language that language could assert no truth'.

Words and their reference

Davidson's (1984) arguments about the nature of reference leads us to the final stage of this brief excursion into theories of meaning. He begins a discussion by saying 'It is difficult to see how a theory of meaning can hope to succeed that does not give a central role to the concept of reference'. The problem lies in giving an account of 'what refers to what' in a simple sentence such as 'the sky is blue' and similar indicative assertions. Solutions are attempted by relating 'meaning' and 'truth', a tactic derived from Frege and Tarski. It is the accounts given by Tarski (1944, 1956 and 1967) which have become standard. For Tarski, an explanation of language and meaning had to take the form of specifying the truth conditions of declarative or indicative sentences of the form 'it is the case that . . .' or 'x is y' and although the result has been described by Norris 'as an elaborate tautology' we should be clear about what is being attempted. And that is an explanation of features of language that does not try to take us beyond language into the realm of fact, a world, an experience or a piece of evidence' and the reason for this is the impossibility of giving accounts of such categories except through language. The attempts to do so in empirical epistemology since Locke using the terminology of 'sensations', 'sense data', 'minima sensibilia' and the like, all fail because they attempt to go behind language but all that was produced were second order statements such that 'when I see an 'x', I have the experience of 'y' sensations' or whatever, depending upon the particular terminology adopted. But such alleged analyses in a second order language did not convey what was actually seen and that had to be expressed in first order terms as 'an x' where 'x' was a member of an ordinary descriptive category such as a 'tree', 'bird' or whatever. It was standardly said that 'we see things as', that is to say, as already conceptualised. The richness of our observations or perceptions, depends upon the richness of our conceptual repertoire and this is acquired in the now familiar phrase 'within a linguistic community'. It is a product of our 'education'.

Tarski expresses what is required to make a sentence 'true' and to have 'meaning' in a formula which sharpens the above account. What he calls convention T, requires 'a satisfactory theory of truth for language L must entail, for every sentence s of L, a theorem of the form s is true if and only if P where ^c s is replaced by a description of s and p by s itself if L is English and by a translation of s into English if L is not English'. (Tarski, 1956). Davidson (1984) observes of this that it is not a definition of 'truth' but it 'represents our best intention as to how the concept of truth is used' and, he continues 'there does not seem to be much hope for a test that a conceptual scheme is radically different from ours if that test depends on the assumption that we can divorce the notion of truth from that of translation'.

Put more succinctly, Tarski's convention T boils down to '"snow white" is true if and only if snow is white' and it works by putting the proposition embodied in the sentence 'snow is white' in quotation marks and the conditions which make it true are disquotational. The 'truth conditions' are of course a specification of what 'snow is white' means. We have therefore a theory of truth which is also a theory of meaning, and it is a specification for correct usage, and a description of usage. In understanding the meaning of a sentence as the way it is used, we also know the conditions which make it 'true'. Its 'truth conditions' are its criteria of meaning.

The merit of such schema is, as I have indicated, that there is no metaphysical 'fact' to be accounted for, for we are in Davidson's terminology functioning within a total conceptual scheme and a system of beliefs. It is infinitely extendable as when new discoveries about the universe are made and 'new' subatomic particles are discovered but each in turn is 'discovered' and described (or named) within the existing scheme, and within which significance and meaning is created. Kripke (1982) prefers to talk in terms of 'assertibility' and 'justificatory' conditions rather than 'truth conditions' and he dispenses with the idea of 'correspondence with facts'. All that is required to legitimize an assertion, is that there be roughly specifiable circumstances under which they are legitimately assertible and that the game of asserting them has a role in our lives'.

Wittgenstein (1953) dismissed the idea of truth conditions by arguing that 'what a proposition is, is in one sense determined by the rules of sentence formation (in English for example) and in another sense by the use of the sign in the language game'. Our understanding of the meaning of a word 'follows from knowing how it is used and this has been learned by learning the rules governing its use'. This view does not contradict the 'truth conditional' argument but it extends it by including the whole range of language games which includes 'asserting', 'giving orders', 'reporting', 'explaining', 'describing', 'asking', 'thanking', 'greeting', 'cursing' and so on. Their respective rules are all generated publicly within what we keep referring to as 'linguistic communities' which legitimise the rules.

Such language is likely to meet with hostility from those who react against concepts such as 'legitimating' and 'privileging' of some statements. On the other hand it is difficult to explain communication except in public terms simply because it is communication between parties, and each party needs to know the conditions which make communication possible. 'Private meanings' are not communicable, and to return to Grice's emphasis upon 'intention', we each choose which language game suits one's purpose, context by context. We choose syntactical forms, grammatical moods and a vocabulary which others will also understand. If we do not do these things we cannot converse and whether we like it or not 'conversation' is a rational, rule governed and value laden activity. We may prefer to be in one community rather than another but we cannot be outside all communities unless we choose to be like Robinson Crusoe.

Reflection should demonstrate how dependent we are upon 'truth telling' in everyday situations. In planning a journey we rely on the information given about train times, we rely on the correctness of instructions on the use of equipment and so on, and we frequently say 'is that true?' 'is that so?' or 'is that right?' and such expressions make no sense unless criteria govern the assertions to which we are responding.

Some Implications

If the general argument of this essay is accepted, we do not, and cannot, reject the idea of 'rationality' per se although new criteria might develop. In fact we have already moved on from the solipsism implied in Cartesian method. The emphasis is now upon the public or social dimension of thought and communication. Language and the development of linguistic skills and abilities becomes more important. This raises important issues in adult education if it is seen as having a major concern for the development of individuality as expressed in terms such as 'personal development'. This is an idea with many dimensions but language must be an important one because it defines us as human beings and moreover as social beings.

Political values are involved, but the liberal concept of individuality does not necessarily imply 'individualism', indeed its own logic precludes it. 'Mutuality' is implicit in the theory of a social contract. But these issues have already been addressed in previous essays, and our present concern is with 'rationality' and 'mutuality' as they appear in language and the ways in which we relate to the world, conceptually and therefore linguistically, and in communication processes and procedures. These activities are by definition not carried out in a social vacuum, and in isolation. In order to 'think' and 'communicate' an element of stability in the system is necessary, and it is difficult to visualise a social system in which 'meaning' was 'free floating'. In order to communicate, a knowledge of 'codes' is a necessary condition and although concepts and linguistic practices might evolve over time, some reference points are fixed and it is from there that 'differences' can be charted as they develop. There is an analogy in 'art' which allows experiment in modes of expression, but art has traditions which provide the reference points which enable us to ask the question 'but is this art?' in situations where the limits of communication are reached. It might do no harm to say e.g. that in art 'anything goes' but what might the response and the consequences be if progression took place and that dead human bodies were used instead of sheep in a work of art?

Communication and the ethical merge at this point and define acceptable limits, not on artistic grounds but on ethical grounds. A failure to communicate might not itself be regarded as important in the case of art if it is seen as an expressive activity, but this marks it out as a limiting case which divides the visual from the literary arts and perhaps music also.

9
'Intention' and the concept of self-directed learning

Introduction

In this concluding essay we return to the concept of 'intention' in order to extend the analysis in ways which would have over-complicated the discussion on rationality and meaning. In a sense therefore it is an appendix to the previous essay and it also relates to the discussion on 'autonomy'. Taken together, the concepts of 'intention' and 'autonomy' are seen as fundamental to an understanding of what is involved in being a 'person' and an 'individual', deemed to be capable of independent thought and action. By relating 'intention' to 'reference' and 'meaning', thought is related to 'action' because in acting 'in the world' we require a capacity to make assumptions which we believe to be 'true'.

These are issues of general philosophical interest and they are relevant to all types of education but they are of particular significance in adult education where 'intentionality' is embodied in the concept of 'self-directed learning'. This has been described as one of the few 'core concepts' which characterise adult education and Tennant expresses it in the following terms:

'At one end of the spectrum "self-directed" learning is thought to occur when learners determine goals and objectives, locate appropriate resources, plan their learning strategies, and evaluate the outcomes. Thus, self-directed learners would be characterised by the mastery of a set of techniques and procedures for self-learning. The other end of the spectrum incorporates the notion of 'critical awareness.' (M Tennant 1991.)

The concept of 'self-direction' has its roots in psychological theory which postulates a 'need' to be self-directing, and continues Tennant, 'an assumption is made that constraints on learning originate in the social structure and become internalized by the adult learner. Shedding these constraints or psychocultural assumptions (according to Mezirow 1985) is at once an act of learning and psychological growth in its own right and a precondition for subsequent self-directed learning'.

'Self-directed learning' is one example of intentional behaviour but there are many others. We are behaving intentionally when we perform a range of quite commonplace actions such as eating our breakfast, engaging in conversation and so on but these kinds of activity are probably so habituated that we do not think of them as 'intentional' although we might describe them as 'voluntary' contrasted with say getting out of bed when the alarm clock rings which might be intentional but not 'voluntary'. Attending an adult education class is probably done both intentionally *and* voluntarily. None of these examples however are of adult educational significance, although some of them might have been so at an earlier stage in learning. In some sense, all adults learn for themselves on the basis of accumulating experience. Nevertheless, the concept of 'self-directed learning' goes beyond this. It is concerned with conscious, goal directed learning and it is more precisely defined. H B Long (1991) says this of it:

> 'The persistence of self-directed learning as a topic of adult education knowledge is explained by several factors. First as with andragogy, the concept is philosophically attractive to adult educators. It focuses on the learner rather than the teacher and ascribes positive (adult) characteristics to the learner. Second, it recognises an idea that many adult educators have long subscribed to: that their role is to develop self-directing learners whose dependence on and need for a teacher is reduced over time'.

There is an extensive literature on the subject and the following schematic procedure, based on an analysis by T M Herman (1977) indicates what is involved in a self-directed learning process. It is formulated as a series of questions to be answered by a hypothetical learner or by a tutor acting on behalf of a learner.

1)   What are we trying to achieve, how do we define our purpose?
2)   On what grounds is it a valid purpose?
3)   What knowledge is required and what is known already that is relevant?
4)   What criteria for assessing learning outcomes are appropriate?

A modified version which substitutes 'action' for 'learning' might well apply to a typical intentional action. Given that much self-directed learning theory is derived from psychological assumptions it seems appropriate to begin by considering 'intention' as a 'mental state'.

'Intention' as a mental state

We are dealing with an ambiguous concept and it has often been described as referring to a 'mental state' (see e.g. Putnam 1981, Grice 1956) but the concept of a 'mental state' is as ambiguous as 'intention' itself, yet we use them both. This reference to 'use' provides a clue to the route which we shall follow in attempting to explain these concepts and it is difficult to see what other possibility is available, and this example illustrates why linguistic analysis has become so pervasive in some branches of philosophy. There appears to be no other way of elucidating non-empirical concepts, unless as in the case of 'mental' concepts they are reduced to behaviourist terms. It might be objected, and with some justification, that in reducing mental concepts to language, and then explaining 'language' in term of use, we are engaging in such reductionism. In the ideas of Grice and Austin for example, as we have indicated in the previous essay 'speech' is 'action'.

From the viewpoint of a discussion of 'rationality' a 'mental state' or a 'state of mind' might seem to be neutral in relation to the concept of 'rationality' and a 'state of mind' might be reduced to the same status as 'desires', 'wishes' or 'wants'. This produces a non-rational premise from which 'reasoning' starts.

The ambiguity inherent in 'states of mind' can be seen in differences in the grammatical forms in which the idea is embedded. Thus typical answers to 'Can you explain your state of mind?' might include 'I am worried, anxious, agitated, calm, happy, contented' and so on. These are all adjectival and a 'state of mind' is expressed by describing how I feel, and this is a strictly private state not accessible by a second person except by observing behaviour, facial expressions and so on. We are dealing with a paradigm mental concept.

In present tense verb forms 'states of mind' are described in the active mode such as 'I am thinking, anticipating, worrying, calculating, planning', etc. In the past tense 'I remembered, recalled, or predicted that', are reflexive forms. They are more accurately described as 'mental actions or processes'. But 'I am intending to . . .' and 'It is my intention to' or 'I intend' are anticipatory - they lead to actions, or rather they might or could do so and this makes them irreducible to anticipated actions.

An attempt to translate 'intentional states' into 'intentional stances' has been discussed recently by Stone (1996) who discusses an earlier theory put forward by Dennett (1982).

On Dennett's argument, what might be described as a 'mental state' may be translated as having *adopted*, or *taken* up an 'intentional stance' a passive form is changed into an active form. The stance is taken or adopted by having reasons for taking that stance and the reasons themselves might be expressed as 'having a belief' or 'believing that . . .', 'having a wish or a desire' and as the result of rationally considering possible ways of achieving a wish, or a desire or of 'acting' on the strength of a belief. It might be asked whether institutions can also have 'intentions' as they have 'goals', 'objectives' and 'purposes', and if the answer is 'yes' this rules out the necessity for introducing mental concepts into the argument. Dennett however, is quoted as saying that institutional systems (i.e. as rational agencies) do not *'really* have beliefs and desires, but that one can explain and predict their behaviour by *ascribing* beliefs and desires to them'. In other words they 'exhibit' intentionality, but the language is metaphorical. Mental concepts as an explanation of personal intentions are not ruled out by this move.

Stone asks 'Does our capacity to adopt the intentional stance presuppose mastery of the concepts 'belief, desire etc.? Or does our mastery of these concepts require or presuppose the capacity to adopt an intentional stance?' Stone argues that if we start from a capacity to adopt an intentional stance there must be a prior understanding of intentional state concepts which leads to the adopting of an intentional stance. (Otherwise we could not know that it *was* an intentional stance). On the other hand, if 'beliefs' provide the starting point as the *reason* for adopting an intentional stance derived from intentional states, we must already possess a concept of an 'intentional state'.

'Intention' as 'prediction' and 'action'

Dennett goes on to argue that a belief 'can be discerned only from the point of view of one who adopts a certain predictive strategy' (a synonym for) 'the intentional stance'. 'To intend' is thus equated with 'to predict' that one will do *particular* things and probably achieve *particular* ends. Against this, Stone claims that the adopting of a stance, or rather having the capacity to do so enables us 'to make sense of intentional state concepts' but a 'stance' is a public expression of a 'state' not its equivalent. This leads us to conclude that none of the arguments lead to a precise description of what a person does 'while adopting an intentional stance', and that 'a full description of the *behaviour* of someone who adopts the stance' leads us to a Wittgenstein style description of a 'form of life', as a set of shared practices.

What we are in need of is a convincing theory of action which bridges the gap between what we wish to do and the doing of it. An alternative to the arguments outlined above, or at least an alternative way of expressing them may be found in theories of 'the will'. One example is in the philosophy of David Hume writing in 1758, another in the writings of Wittgenstein.

In the terminology of 'intentional stances' the adoption of a stance is manifest in the performance of an action that we are able and willing to perform. In the terminology of 'willing' to act is to demonstrate a 'will' to act. This may be illustrated negatively as when we say 'I intended to do so and so today but I never got around to doing it'. This demonstrates a lack of will, or it is taken as an indication of someone who is 'weak willed'. Nevertheless explaining what is meant by a 'will' or an 'act of willing' is not easy. The problem is to explain how a free agent with wishes, desires and intentions moves from the mental state of taking a stance in the sense of having a commitment, to a physical action. (For this purpose, a speech act is partly a physical action using our vocal chords). In modern parlance a control system is required which links thought, feelings (such as desires, wishes etc.) and action in ways that make it our voluntary, intended action. Such a system can be hypothesised in terms of 'willing' and the possession of 'a will' which in some way takes over when a 'stance' is translated into action.

It might be objected that by introducing new concepts such as 'will' and 'acts of willing' we are proliferating unnecessary mental entities and processes, therefore in order to meet this objection they must be shown to be of practical as well as philosophical value. What the vocabulary of 'will' does in respect of self-directed learning is to take us beyond the limits of learned techniques and procedures. Attention is focused upon affective and attitudinal aspects of 'self-direction' where a *desire* to be self-directed might have to be engendered alongside the acquisition of techniques and the mastery of procedures. For adults who are not accustomed to the idea of freedom to choose within education or in their working environment, the attitudinal dimension might be critical. Hume (1758 and 1951) makes this point rather well when he says 'It is certain that the easy and obvious philosophy will always, with the generality of mankind, have the preference above the accurate and abstruse'. Doing what others do, or acting on instructions might for some be the 'easier' philosophy. As Fromme pointed out 'freedom' can be feared.

For Hume 'the will' is not *under* our command, it is that which *enables* us to command ourselves to act, the latter not being the same thing as (involuntarily) 'behaving'. In Hume's view 'intentions' depend on 'belief' which lie 'in some sentiment or feeling . . . which depends not on the will, nor can be commanded at pleasure. It must be excited by nature like all other sentiments and arise from the particular situation in which the mind is placed at any particular juncture'. This suggests that context influences or generates beliefs which are contingent on circumstances. 'Belief' in Hume's terminology is a 'feeling'. This means that it is beyond conscious control, and it is beyond reason. We do not arrive at beliefs, we simply 'have them'. Nevertheless we 'believe that' or 'believe in' something. Beliefs are reflexively expressed and this implies conceptualisation. Thus says Hume 'belief is nothing but a more vivid, lively, forcible, firm, steady conception of an object'. This formulation implies that a belief *is* a conceptualisation rather than an attitude towards a conceptualisation. Thus to say 'I am writing' is itself an expression of belief as an awareness of what I am now doing but my belief may be either 'true' or 'false'. It is not necessarily true because I might be mistakenly describing what (from the point of view of an observer) I am actually doing. Beliefs are not self-justifying. We turn meanwhile to Wittgenstein's accounts of 'will'. As does Hume, he places the discussion in the context of the 'mind controlling the body' as a paradigm of a 'voluntary action, which is also an intentional action'. In the 'Brown Book' (1958) he states that:

'The problem that we are concerned with we also encounter in thinking about volition, deliberate and involuntary action. Think say of these examples: I *deliberate* whether to lift a certain heavyish weight and *decide* to do it. I then *apply* my force to it and *lift* it'. (My italics). These are four distinct acts, and Wittgenstein suggests that this might be seen as a 'full fledged case of willing and intentional action'. But this would be misleading. 'We speak', he claims of 'an act of volition' as different from the action which is willed. This in my terminology above is equivalent to arriving at an intentional stance and then acting. For Dennett, it is translation into an active form from an inactive 'mental state'.

The correlation of 'willing' with 'mental states' is the problem and as we noted above, Grice and Austin reduce 'mental states' to action when discussing language. For them 'speech is action'. This is a Wittgensteinian view and he is trying to detach us from unnecessary postulations of 'mental states', his view is succinctly expressed in the simple question ' . . . when I raise my arm, my arm goes up. And the problem arises: what is left over if I subtract the fact that my arm goes up from the fact that I raise my arm?' (Wittgenstein 1963, para 621). His answer effectively is 'nothing' and in para 615 he has already said 'willing' if it is not to be a sort of wishing *must be the action itself*. (My italics). It indicates that we have done what we wanted when we say 'I willed the action'.

This discussion might seem to have taken us a long way from 'intention' and 'self-directed learning' and we have apparently finished up with a behavioural account, but it is not quite that. It also indicates that the claim to be self-directed *is* to say 'that we did what we wanted to do'. It also implies that we had the *confidence* to make such a claim and that as a consequence we enjoy the *dignity* of being self-directing. The whole concept of 'self-direction' might be justified in terms of the status it confers on adult learners. That is its major objective.

Reference, truth and meaning
The discussion now leads back to the problems of reference, truth and meaning, which were discussed in the previous essay. It does so in order to remind us what we said and in order to make a few additional points. They may be placed in the context of intentionality and self-directed learning because they underpin the schematic list of questions set out above. 'References, truth and meaning', are embedded in thought, the idea of knowledge and in communication. If a tutor for example suggests that a given area of learning is consistent with the

learners own purpose, there must be understanding of and trust in, the validity of the advice given. 'Truth' might be treated as an abstruse philosophical subject, but it plays a very practical role. It is the foundation of mutual trust by providing an *acceptable* justification for what is said and recommended. What is meant by 'truth' in a given context presupposes a theory of truth and a set of agreed 'truth conditions' which warrant application of the term 'truth'. There are many theories of truth but as a working concept it is indispensable. To what do our statements refer in order to satisfy Tarski style truth conditions? If 'y' intend that 'x' there must be an assumption that 'x' is in some sense beyond my 'self'. I do not merely wish or intend to go on 'thinking that' *ad infinitum*. I wish to influence the world in some way by acting in it, yet that world is also acting on me.

Putnam (1981) reminds us that 'some philosophers' (most famously Brentano) have ascribed to the mind a power of 'intentionality' which precisely enables it to refer. That is to say to make contact with the world. But it is difficult to give an account which does not make use of the idea of a 'concept' and that when we see an object such as a 'house' or a 'tree' we see it as a token of the concept of a house, a tree or whatever actual object we refer to. This means that when the truth conditional for 'The cat is on the mat' is satisfied, the cat must be on the mat, the conditions for the correct application of a sentence are satisfied, i.e. its 'meaning' conditions are satisfied, but no explanation has been given. If a sentence such as 'the cat is on the mat' is true, if and only if the cat is on the mat what are we to make of the disquotational sentence? The vocabulary of 'concepts' as in 'I have a concept of' appears to be in the realm of 'mental state' which is itself a 'concept'. Putnam makes use of two categories of 'mental state'.

1)   A *pure* mental state which refers only to 'what goes on "inside" the speaker'. Examples of the kind noted above such as 'anxiety', 'fear', 'pain' etc. are in this category. Of these, it makes no sense to say that we 'know' that we are 'anxious', 'happy' or whatever. These just *are* the states that we are or could be 'in'.

2)   consists of cases where a knowledge and claim is made. There is a mental component but that results from there being something outside which leads a person to believe that something is the case and what we call 'knowledge' makes a claim that the belief is 'true'.

In speaking about 'the world' by asserting 'that x' Putnam uses the device of 'bracketing' thus my belief 'that x' is a bracketed belief that [there is x]. The bracketed belief is an impure belief reflecting an intention (in the Brentano sense) that the term 'x' refers to a real x, and it is this type of argument which led Davidson to claim that we share 'a picture of the world that in its large features must be true'. If it were not so, he argues, it is difficult to explain how so much of what we intend turns out to be possible. We can actually do things so much of what we intend turns out to be possible. We can actually do things such as sending men to the moon as well as many more mundane tasks. Davidson (1974 and 1984) gives a cautious explanation of 'truth' as correct response or correspondence 'by appeal to a relation between language and the world and *that* analysis of that relation yields insight into how by allowing sentences, one *sometimes* manages to say what is true' (my italics). The arguments makes use of technical logical devices but the conclusion is 'Statements are true or false because of the words used in making them, and it is these words that have interesting, detailed, conversational connections with the world'. 'Truth (in a given language) is (however) not a property of sentences: it is a relation between sentences, speakers and dates', (which) 'invite the construction of a *theory*' (my italics).

Conceptual Schemes

In the preceding section, use was made of Putnam's argument that 'intentionality' cannot be explained as a 'pure' mental state if it enables us to make contact with the world. It is impossible to do this simply by being a 'power in the mind'. Something beyond the self is required and use is made of 'concepts', which in Davidson's terms enable us 'to share a picture of the world'. The metaphor of a 'picture' is also expressible as 'a conceptual scheme'. This can be described as a system of categories which in some sense are used to 'organise our experience' but this way of putting it assumes a dualism between an 'unorganised' and an 'organised' experience after the fashion of empiricism presented in terms such as 'sense data', 'raw feels' and so on. For Putnam, 'meanings' are not 'just in the head', they are, in Grice's and Wittgenstein's sense, generated by using words, but in order to communicate, there must be limits to the use and meaning of particular words. There need not be a single rule for 'correct use' but some agreement is necessary, especially in the use of concepts, although there are cases of having different concepts with the same sign or name as in the case of 'space'. Putnam explains 'how the reference of our terms is fixed, given that it is not fixed simply by our mental states' in the following way.

'In logic the set of things a term is true of is called the *extension* of the term'. Thus the extension of the term 'cat' is the set of 'cats'.

The *intention* is the set of possible objects which is associated with the term 'cat'. For our present purpose this is settled by what we call 'definition' which determines what shall be regarded as a member of a set.

Davidson argues that 'we may identify conceptual schemes with languages and that the possibility of translation between languages is evidence that they share the same conceptual schemes. But in saying this, he confines us within language and there appears to be no explanation of the way in which concepts connect to 'the world'. We cannot deal with the long-standing question about the possibility of distinguishing between conceptual scheme and empirical content. There is no 'logical' space for such a distinction. An explanation might be provided by dropping the assumption that a once for all solution is possible from a static position, whereas no human being comes to such a question from nowhere. Languages and concepts are learned over a period of time, and each individual enters a tradition within which languages and concepts have developed. We already 'see' a world as it is conceptualised, and it reflects assumptions, values, intentions and purposes as a 'given' but from which development takes place as in the model of the sciences. Familiar terms acquire new meaning, and new terms are introduced to explain new data. Understanding and communication is being portrayed in a pragmatic way as reflecting intentions and in turn shaping new intentions. 'Truth' becomes a semantic notion and as Davidson puts it 'Of course the truth of sentences remains relative to language but that is as objective as we can be'.

Knowledge and beliefs as shared and provisional

In sum, a prevailing view is that 'language, truth and meaning' are interrelated notions embedded in a total system of concepts and beliefs which together enable *us in concert* with one another to comprehend, communicate and act upon shared *beliefs* in shared languages. Knowledge has become corporate, and language is conventional, pragmatic but ordered and it enables us to feel our way forward as best we can. In a sense, knowledge is theoretical, probable and reviewable. We correct errors and revise theory when it fails to work. We operate with paradigm examples and change the paradigms when they fail in too many instances and the ways in which scientists especially, do this, forms the subject of Kuhn's (1962) Theory of Scientific Revolutions. His argument has been criticised partly on the grounds that he is imprecise about the nature of paradigms and paradigm shifts. Newtonian physics for example have not been rejected. They apply adequately in some circumstances but not others, and new theories develop and are used in circumstances in which they have the most explanatory power and the best predictive results. But it should be emphasised that when new data is observed or collected, it is first fitted into or 'tried for fit' as it were in existing theories as when sub-atomic particles are discovered and fitted into incomplete equations which give them significance.

At a different level we do the same with everyday data which is incorporated into a variety of linguistic structures thus we learn to describe artifacts, experience, and new intensions using literal and metaphoric, language, we formulate new indicative, assertiorial and expressive sentences of infinite diversity, generating them from a common stock of shared languages, within which shared values are embedded. It is not the task of philosophy to change language but, as Wittgenstein said, to describe it, to which we might add 'and to explain how it functions'. What are called 'semantic theories of meaning and truth' are one attempt to explain, and at the present time they appear to be the most satisfying that we have but they are revisable and might be superseded. What they show is that it is impossible to escape the conclusion that language is a corporate medium and that we cannot isolate ourselves as solipsists.

'Self-direction' therefore has to be understood within a framework which *is* a constraint as Mezirow claims in the sense that 'intention' is expressed within already learned languages and existing conceptual schemes. But as we saw in the earlier essays we function within traditions within which change is possible, but it is not within the control of any single individual, although some appear to have more influence than others. We are not all 'seminal thinkers', although those who are called such also start from within a tradition to which we each contribute and perhaps in some degree modify, in the process of learning from what is beyond ourselves. But the process of learning involves an interpretation and translation into our own concepts and fund of knowledge previously acquired. Thus we are involved in a dual process of being shaped by what is learned, but our experiences may be seen as shaping what is learned as it also becomes a part of our experiences. From this point of view, whether or not learning is self-directed, seems to be less important than the act of learning.

Bibliography

ACACE (1982). *Continuing Education: From Policies to Practice*. Advisory Council for Adult and Continuing Education.

Allman, P. and Wallis, J. (1995). 'Gramsci's Challenge to the Politics of the Left in "Our Times"', *International Journal of Lifelong Education* Vol. 14, No. 2.

Ayer, A.J. (1958). *The Problem of Knowledge*. London: MacMillan.

Beck, A.W. (1971) 'Does "Ethics and Education" rest on a mistake?', *Educational Philosophy and Theory* Vol. 3, No. 2.

Black, M. (1967). 'Rules and Routines' in *The Concept of Education* (ed. R.S. Peters). London: Routledge.

Bowers, C.A. (1983). 'Linguistic Roots of Cultural Invasion in Paulo Freire's Pedagogy', *Teachers' Record* Vol. 84, No 4.

Bowers, C.A. (1986). 'Review of the Politics of Education, Culture and Power', *Educational Studies* Vol. 17, No 1.

Bright, B. (ed.) (1989). *Theory and Practice in the Study of Adult Education*. London and New York: Routledge.

Davidson, D. (1984). *Inquiries into Truth and Interpretation*. Oxford University Press.

Davidson, D. (1967). 'Truth and Meaning', *Synthese* XVII.

Dennett, D. (1978). *Brainstorms*. Montgomery, USA: Bradford Books.

Den Vyl and Rasmusson (1981). 'Nozick on the Random Argument' in *Reading Nozick* (ed. Paul Jeffrey). Oxford: Basil Blackwell.

Dworkin, R.M. (1977). 'Is law a system of rules' in *The Philosophy of Law* (ed. R M Dworkin). Oxford University Press.

Dworkin, R.M. (1986). *A Matter of Principle*. Oxford University Press.

Edwards, R. and Usher, R. (1995). 'Confessing All? A Postmodern Guide to the Guidance and Counselling of Adult Learners', *Studies in the Education of Adults* Vol. 27, No. 1.

Elias, J.L. and Merriam, S. (1980). *Philosophical Foundations of Adult Education*. New York: Krieger.

Farrar, C. (1988). *The Origins of Democratic Thinking*. Cambridge University Press.

Goodman, N. (1977). *The Structure of Appearance* (third edition). Amsterdam, Boston, and London: Reidel Publishing.

Gombrich, E.H. (1959). *Art and Illusion*. Oxford: Phaidon Press.

Grice, P.H. (1967). 'Meaning', *The Philosophical Review* Vol. 66, July.

Grice, P.H. (1968). 'Utterers Meaning, Sentence Meaning', *Foundations of Language* Vol. 4, August.

Grice, P.H. (1979). 'The John Locke Lectures'. Unpublished. Quoted in *Philosophical Grounds of Rationality* (eds. R.E. Grandy and R. Warner, 1988). Oxford: Clarendon.

Griffin, C. 'Curriculum theory' in *Adult and Lifelong Education*. London: Croom Helm.

Hacker, P.M.S. (1996). 'On Davidson's Idea of a Conceptual Scheme', *Philosophical Quarterly* Vol. 46, No. 184.

Hart, L.A. (1977). 'Positivism and the separation of law and morals' in *The Philosophy of Law* (ed. R.M. Dworkin). Oxford University Press.

Hamilton, A. (1995). 'A New Look at Personal Identity', *Philosophical Quarterly* Vol. 45, No. 180, July.

Heal, J. (1990). 'Pragmatism and Choosing to Believe' in *Reading Rorty* (ed. A. Malachowski) Oxford: Blackwell.

Hegel, (1821 and 1952). *Philosophy of Right*. Translated T.M. Know. Oxford: Clarendon Press.

Heller, A. (1987). *Beyond Justice*. Oxford: Blackwell.

Herman, T.M. (1977). *Creative Learning Environments: The Behavioural Approach to Education*. Boston: Allyn and Bacon.

Hirst, P.H. (1965). 'Liberal education and the nature of knowledge' in *Philosophical Analysis and Education* (ed. R D Archambault). London: Routledge and Kegan Paul.

Hirst, P.H. (1974). *Knowledge and the Curriculum.* London: Routledge and Kegan Paul.

Hirst, P.H. (1983). 'Educational theory' in *Educational Theory and its Foundation Disciplines* (ed. Hirst). London: Routledge and Kegan Paul.

James, W. (1917). *William James. Selected Papers on Philosophy.* London and New York: European Library, J.M. Dent and Sons Ltd.

Jensen, G., Liveright, A.A. and Hallenbeck, W. (eds.) (1964). *Adult Education. Outlines of an Emerging Field of University Study.* Adult Education Association of the USA.

Kallen, H. (1962). *Philosophical Issues in Adult Education.* Illinois: Charles Thomas.

Keddie, N. (1980). 'Adult education: an ideology of individualism' in *Adult Education for a Change* (ed. Jane Thompson). London: Hutchinson.

Kitto, H.D.F. (1964). *The Greeks.* Harmondsworth, England: Penguin Books.

Kripke, S.A. (1982). *Wittgenstein on Rules and Private Language.* Oxford: Blackwell.

Kuhn, T.S. (1970). *The Structure of Scientific Revolutions* (second edition). Chicago University Press.

Langford, G. (1979 and 1985). *Educating Persons and Society.* London: Macmillan.

Lawson, K.H. (1979). *Philosophical Concepts and Values in Adult Education.* Milton Keynes: Open University.

Lawson, K.H. (1982). *Analysis and Ideology: Conceptual Essays on the Education of Adults.* University of Nottingham, Department of Adult Education.

Lawson, K.H. (1985). 'Deontological liberalism: the political philosophy of liberal adult education', *International Journal of Lifelong Education* Vol. 4, No. 3, pp.219-227.

Lawson, K.H. (1987). 'Liberal education, rule governed behaviour and legal philosophy', *International Journal of Lifelong Education* Vol. 6, No. 2, pp.103-110.

Lowe, J. (1970). *Adult Education in England and Wales.* London: Michael Joseph.

Locke, J. (1690 and 1956). 'Second Treatise on Civil Government' in *Social Contract* (ed. Sir Ernest Barker). Oxford University Press.

Long, H.B. (1991). 'Evolution of a Formal Knowledge Base' in *Adult Education* (J.M. Peters and P. Jarvis and Associates). San Francisco: Josey Bass.

Lyotard, J.F. (1979). *The Postmodern Condition*. Translated G. Bennington, and B. Massomi. Manchester University Press.

MacIntyre, A. (1981). *After Virtue*. London: Duckworth.

MacIntyre, A. (1988). *Whose Justice, Which Rationality?* London: Duckworth.

Mezirow, J. (1985). *A Critical Theory of Self-Directed Learning*. San Francisco: Josey-Bass.

Mill, J.S. (1861 and 1962). *Utilitarianism* (ed. Warnock). London: Fontana Press.

Nagel, T. (1982). 'Libertarianism Without Foundations' in *Reading Nozick* (ed. Paul Jeffrey). Oxford: Blackwell.

National Institute of Adult Continuing Education (annually). *Year Book of Adult Continuing Education.* Leicester.

Norriss, C. (1988). *Deconstruction and the Critique of Ideology.* London: Routledge.

Nozick, R. (1974). *Anarchy, State and Utopia.* Oxford: Basil Blackwell.

Nozick, R. (1981). 'On the Randian Argument' in *Reading Nozick* (ed. Jeffrey Paul). Oxford: Basil Blackwell.

Paterson, R.W.K. (1979). *Values, Education and the Adult.* London: Routledge and Kegan Paul.

Paterson, R.W.K. (1995). 'Liberal Adult Education in the Twenty-First Century' in *Liberal Adult Education: End of an Era?* (ed. J. Wallis). University of Nottingham: Continuing Education Press.

Peters, R.S. (1966). *Ethics and Education.* London: George Allen and Unwin.

Peters, R.S. (1967). 'What is an educational process?' in *The Concept of Education* (ed. R.S. Peters). London: Routledge and Kegan Paul.

Peters, R.S. (1967). 'Freedom and the Development of the Free Man' in *Educational Judgements* (ed. J.F. Doyle). London: Routledge and Kegan Paul.

Plecas, D.B. and Stork, T.J. (1986). 'Adult education: Curing the ills of an undisciplined discipline', *Adult Education Quarterly* Vol. 37, No. 1.

Popper, K. (1956). *The Logic of Scientific Discovery.* London: Hutchinson.

Putnam, H. (1981). *Reason Truth and History.* Cambridge University Press.

Putman, H. (1983). *Realism and Reason.* Cambridge University Press.

Quine, M. V. (1953). *From a Logical Point of View*. Cambridge, Massachussets: Harvard University Press.

Rawls, J. (1973). *A Theory of Justice*. Oxford University Press.

Roberts, P. (1996). 'Rethinking Conscientisation', *Journal of Philosophy of Education* Vol. 30, Issue 2.

Rorty, R. (1979). *Philosophy and the Mirror of Nature*. University of Princeton.

Rorty, R. (1987) 'Pragmatism and philosophy' in *After Philosophy: End or Transformation* (eds. K. Baynes, J. Bohman and T. McCarthy). Cambridge, Massachusetts and London: The MIT Press.

Ryle, G. (1967). *The Concept of Mind*. London: Hutchinson.

Sabine, G.H. (1949). *A History of Political Theory*. London: Harrap.

Sandel, M.J. (1982). *Liberalism and the Limits of Justice*. Cambridge University Press.

Schick, F. (1984). *Having Reasons: An Essay on Rationality and Sociality*. Princeton University Press.

Schroeder, W.L. (1970). 'Adult Education Described and Defined' in *Handbook of Adult Education* (eds. Smith, Aker and Kidd). New York: MacMillan.

Slors, M. (1996). 'Why Dennett Cannot Explain What it is to Adopt a Traditional Stance', *Philosophical Quarterly* Vol. 46, No. 182.

Tarski, A. (1944). 'The Semantic Conception of Truth', *Philosophy and Phenomenological Research* 4.

Tarski, A. (1956). 'The Concept of Truth in Formalised Languages' in *Logic, Semantics and Mathematics*. Oxford: Clarendon Press.

Taylor, C. (1991). *The Ethics of Authenticity*. Cambridge, Massachusetts and London: Harvard University Press.

Tennant, M. (1991). 'The Psychology of Adult Teaching and Learning' in *Adult Education* (J.M. Peters, P. Jarvis and Associates). San Francisco: Josey Bass.

Toulmin, S. (1950). *Reason in Ethics*. Cambridge University Press.

Thompson, J. L. (1980). *Adult Education For A Change*. Hutchinson.

Williams, B., 1995, 'Replies' in *World, Mind and Ethics* (eds. J.E.J. Altham and R. Harrison). Cambridge University Press.

Wiltshire, H. C. (1964). *The Nature and Uses of Adult Education*. University of Nottingham, Department of Adult Education.

Wiltshire, H.C. (1976). *The Spirit and the Form* (ed. A. Rogers). University of Nottingham, Department of Adult Education.

Wittgenstein, L. (1953). *Philosophical Investigations* (second edition). Translated G.E.M. Anscombe (1958). Oxford: Blackwell.

INDEX

ACACE 41
action
  intention as 130-2
  rational 112-15, 118-19
  speech is 129, 132
adult/adulthood 13, 19, 26, 104
adult education 3, 106, 127-36
  conceptualization of 19-32, 104
  liberal 37, 41, 53, 68-70, 83
  personal autonomy and 99-100
analytical philosophy of education
  (APE) 69
analytical style 14-15
andragogy 26, 41, 128
Athenian democracy 57-8, 59-60,
  88
authenticity 65-6
authority 44-5, 116
autonomous persons 33, 38, 69, 86,
  87, 94
autonomy 34, 69, 85, 98-100
  contingency of 95-6
  definitions of 87-8
  as educational objective 23-4,
  25-6
  and intentionality 93-5, 127
  and non-autonomy 85-7
  political concept of 88-90
  Rawls and 38
  reason and 59-60, 85, 86
Ayer, A.J. 90, 96, 122

belief 28, 122, 130, 131, 135-6
  Hume and 131-2
  thought and 119
beneficent liberalism 56, 115
Black, M. 115

choice 34, 43
  in education 70

obligation and 76
  rationality of 60, 80-1, 115
  state and 36, 61
citizenship 58, 71, 72
  as constraint 77-8
  obligation of 78-80
classical liberalism 56
communication 93, 126
  language and 65, 98, 125, 135
  meaning and 118-20
communicative rationality 112
community 24-5, 34, 69
community education 23, 24-5
concepts 27, 29, 107, 111, 122, 133,
  134-5
constraints 37, 64, 86, 115
  citizenship and 77-8
continuing education 23, 25
conventions 100-1, 118
critical theory 14-15
criteria 28, 44-5, 50, 116, 118
cultural norms 92-3
culture 65, 123
curriculum 24, 49

Davidson, D. 106, 108, 122, 123, 124
  134-5
democracy 54, 61, 67
  Athenian 57-8, 59-60, 88
Dennett, D. 129-30
Den Vyl, D. 63-4
deontological principle 71, 72, 75, 82
  see also liberalism, deontological
Descartes, Rene 15, 59, 82-3
descriptive education 46
discussion 55-6, 58
dispositions 74
duties 56
  see also obligation; responsibility
Dworkin, R. 45, 47-8, 49, 54, 66

education 19, 26, 34, 46, 106
    continuing 23, 25
    lifelong 23, 25
    meaning of 20, 21
    see also adult education;
        community education; liberal
        education; recurrent education
Ely, J. 67
English National Institute of Adult
    Education 13
enquiry 50
epistemology 15, 22, 26-7, 29, 50, 123
equality 39, 55, 89
ethics *see* morality

fairness 34, 39, 77, 115
falsification 116, 123
Farrar, C. 57-8, 88
free will 58, 89
freedom 29, 40, 61
    Athenian 57
    Mill and 55-6, 64, 89
    Nagel and 54
    Rawls and 77

Gadamer, H.G. 99
good 37-8, 40, 57, 71
    of others 26, 51, 55
    private and public 33, 60, 62-3
good reasons 81
grammar 116, 118, 120, 122, 125
grammatical forms 129
Grice, P.H. 118-19, 120, 121, 132
Griffin, C. 33

Hacker, P.M.S. 108
Hamilton, A. 91
Hart, H.L.A. 47, 48-9
Heal, J. 94
Hegel, G.W.F. 86, 88
Heller, A. 68
Herman, T.M. 128
Hirst, P.H. 22, 29
Hume, David 130, 131

identity 91-2
immanence 30, 31
imperative and indicative utterances
    119, 120, 121
implication 119-21
importance 79-83
individual/s 13, 37, 38, 40, 61, 64
    choice and 80
    Rawls and 82
    sovereignty of 60
individualism 33, 34, 37, 51, 81
    liberalism and 63-5, 68
    Locke and 35, 37
individuality 15, 68, 74, 81
    and autonomy 90-2
    Locke and 60-1
    Mill and 55-6, 89-90
    and mutuality 14, 71, 125
instruction 24
intention
    as a mental state 128-30
    as prediction and action 130-2
        rational action and 112,
        118, 119
    and self-directed learning 127-36
intentionality 93-5
interests 38-9, 60

judgement/s 48, 64, 77-8, 93, 98
    autonomy and 85, 87
    moral 81-2
    value 113
judicial review 66-7
justice 39-40, 67
    Locke and 36, 38
    Rawls and 37, 62, 115
    see also fairness
justification 112, 113, 115
justificatory claims 27

Kallen, H. 13
Kant, immanuel 38, 75
Keddie, N. 33
Kitto, H.D.F. 58

knowledge 22, 27, 29, 50, 133, 135-6
Kripke, S.A. 96, 124
Kuhn, T.S. 116, 117, 135

Langford, G. 29, 30
language 65, 98, 134-6
   rationality of 117, 118, 125
   translation of 103, 106-9, 134-5
language games 22, 28-9, 59, 73, 96
laws 45-9
Lawson, K.H. 19
learning 41, 103
   choice in 86
   organized 24
   self-directed 127-36
liberal education 43-51
   see also adult education, liberal
liberalism 25-6, 53-4, 55-6, 109-10
   deontological 33-42, 58, 67, 69-70, 73
   Dworkin and 54
   historical roots of 57-8
   individualism and 51
   rationality and 59-65
liberty *see* freedom
Locke, John 15, 33, 35-6, 60, 61
logic 80, 100-1, 114
logical positivism 114, 122
Long, H.B. 128
Lowe, J. 19-20
Lyotard, J.F. 65-6

MacIntyre, A. 53, 64, 72, 106, 109
   and rationality 59, 113, 114, 117
Macpherson, C.B. 61
Marx, Karl 108
Marxism 15, 110
   understanding 107, 108
meaning 105-6, 132-4
   explanation of 107-8
   as intention 105, 118-19
   and reference 123-5
   theories of 31-2
memory 91, 97

mental autonomy 87
mental states 129-30, 131-2, 133, 134
Merriam, S. 13
metaphor 87, 88
Mill, J.S. 59, 69, 80, 86
   and beneficent liberalism 55, 56, 60
   and individuality 89-90
moral conscience 76
moral education 75
morality 38-79
   law and 45-6, 47-9
   of obligation 71-7
   values and 72
mutuality 14, 15, 71, 83, 85, 125

Nagel, T. 54, 55, 60
normative education 46
normative expectations 87-8
Norris, C. 123
Nozick, Richard 33, 34, 36, 37, 61, 62, 63

objectives 73, 99, 132
objectivity 44-5, 121
obligation 45-6, 47
   morality of 71-7
   of citizenship 78-80
observation 26-7

paradigms 31, 32, 117, 118, 135
Paterson, R.W.K. 19, 34, 69, 87, 104
penumbra 48-9
person *see* individual; self
personal preferences 63, 64-5, 70, 114, 115
Peters, R.S. 44, 45, 46, 87
philosophy 22, 31
   of adult education 25, 26-9, 133-42
Plecas, D.B. 20, 22-3, 24
political 15, 57-8, 71-2
   and autonomy 88-90
politics 66-7
   liberal 54, 55, 56
Popper, Karl 116

postmodernism 15, 65, 105
power 15, 44, 47
pragmatic 46, 50, 74
prediction 130-2
private domain 33, 55, 60, 62-3, 80, 90
private language 96-8
privileged 97
property 62
    Locke and 36, 61
Putnam, Hilary 29, 30, 100, 106, 116,
    118, 121-2, 133, 134
puzzle solving 117

Quine, M.V. 100, 106, 122

Radbruch, G. 47
radical adult education 26
Rand, A. 63
Rasmussen, D. 63-4
rational autonomy 43
rational decision 38-9
rationality 15, 45, 81, 111-12
    autonomy and 86
    changing 58-65
    institutionalised 113, 114
    politics and 56
    rational action 112-15
    rule-based 115-16
Rawls, John 33, 61, 82
    and justice 37-9, 62, 77, 115
reason 36, 89, 92
    autonomy and 59-60, 85, 86
recurrent education 23-4, 26
reference 123-5, 132-4
relativism 22, 25, 27-9, 117, 122
    cultural 123
responsibility 81, 116
    autonomy and 86, 87, 88, 93
right to choose 40-1, 62
rights 34, 60, 62
    citizenship 79
    justice and 37, 39
    Locke and 35-6
Rorty, R. 22, 28

rule-governed behaviour 43, 48
rules 43
    and laws 45-7
    and moral obligation 74-5
    rule of law 47-9
    Wittgenstein and 95, 96-8

Sabine, G.H. 58
Sandel, M.J. 39
Schick, F. 114
science 2, 83, 116-18
self 38, 40, 65-6, 70, 72, 90
    see also individual
self-actualisation 13
self-directed learning 127-36
self-interest 74, 75, 113, 115
self-preservation 36, 38
social contract 38-9, 71, 125
society 51, 60, 73, 89
    based on justice 62, 115
    state and 34
Sork, T.S. 20, 22-3, 24
sovereignty 88
    Mill and 60, 89
state 57, 60, 88
    functions of 66
    Locke and 36, 61
    minimal 36-7, 54, 68, 81
    self-interest and 34
style 30, 105
subcultures 27, 31, 103, 106
subjectivity *see* self

Tarski, A. 123, 124
Taylor, C. 65, 66
teaching 24, 30
Tennant, M. 127
theory 22-3, 25, 30, 32, 70, 116, 122, 135
thought 87, 92-3, 119
tradition 30, 99, 103-6
    liberal 59, 68, 69
    translation and 106-9
traditionalists 104
training 31, 106

transcendence 30, 31, 82
translation 31, 106-9
truth 15, 27, 40, 132-4, 135
    language and 108-9
    meaning and 121-3, 124
    truth telling 44, 45, 113, 125

understanding 93, 107-8, 109, 112, 135
universal principles 28
utilitarianism 37-8, 60
values 39-40, 41, 81, 82, 83
    foundational 67-8
    liberal 106
    obligation and 71-2, 78, 79
    plurality of 27, 77
    relativism of 122
    in translation 107
veil of ignorance 39, 61-2, 82
verification 27, 91, 114
vocabulary 32, 95, 105

WEA 19, 26
welfare 56
will 45, 89, 130-2
Williams, B. 72, 73, 75, 76, 79
Wiltshire, H.C. 19, 69